中美合作项目

数字影像——蓝田水陆庵彩绘泥塑群

中国国家文物局、陕西省文物局、美国梅隆基金会出资支持

The Sino-American Collaborations Project

Digital Images of the Painted Clay Sculptures at the Shuilu'an in Lantian

With financial support from the state Administration of Cultural Heritage, the Shaanxi Bureau

of Cultural Relics and the Andrew W. Mellon Foundation

影像水陆庵

IMAGES OF SHUILU'AN

影 像 水 陆 庵

IMAGES OF SHUILU'AN

中国西安文物保护修复中心　美国西北大学学术技术部　著

Jointly produced by the Xi'an Center for the Conservation and Restoration of Cultural Relics
Northwestern University Information Technologies Department of Academic &
Research Technologies Advanced Media Production Studio

文物出版社

北京 · 2009 年

图书在版编目（CIP）数据

影像水陆庵/中国西安文物保护修复中心，美国西北大
学学术技术部著. －北京：文物出版社，2009.10
　ISBN 978-7-5010-2841-2

Ⅰ．影… Ⅱ．①中… ②美… Ⅲ．佛像－石刻造像－蓝田
县－图集 Ⅳ．K879．32

中国版本图书馆 CIP 数据核字（2009）第 167818 号

影像水陆庵

著　者	中国西安文物保护修复中心
	美国西北大学学术技术部
装帧设计	周小玮
责任印制	张道奇
责任编辑	王　戈
出版发行	文物出版社
地　址	北京市东直门内北小街 2 号楼
	邮政编码　100007
	http://www.wenwu.com
	web@wenwu.com

制版印刷	北京燕泰美术制版印刷有限责任公司
经　销	新华书店
版　次	2009 年 10 月第 1 版第 1 次印刷
开　本	787 × 1092　　1/8
印　张	25
书　号	ISBN 978-7-5010-2841-2
定　价	580 元

中美合作项目组

中　方

组长　王道武

成员　王展　杨宝贵　甄刚　李博　阎敏

美　方

组长　哈伦·瓦拉克

成员　庄纳坦·斯密斯　威廉·帕罗德　斯特芳妮·佛斯特　拉尔斯·胡布里克　杰勒米·布伦吉斯
詹姆斯·普林斯　罗兰·何丽戴　吴明宗　林星格文化公司　约瑟夫·帕里斯　克里斯托弗·瓦拉斯
庄纳坦·佛南德斯　梅缵月　郑丽敏　艾黎孙·拉森

Project Teams

The People's Republic of China

Team Leader　Wang Daowu

Team members　Wang Zhan　Yang Baogui　Zhen Gang　Li Bo　Yan Min

United States of America

Team Leader　Harlan Wallach

Team members　Jonathan Smith　Bill Parod　Stefani Foster　Lars Hubrich　Jeremy Brunjes

James Prinz　Lauren Holliday　Mitchell Wu　Linsinger Kultur　Joseph Paris　Christopher Wallace

Jonathan Fernandez　June Mei　Limin Teh　Allison Larsen

编者说明

1. 本书是在中美合作《三维扫描及数字化图像制作技术在蓝田水陆庵的应用研究》项目成果的基础上编辑而成，图书的出版也是项目成果之一。

2. 该项目由中国西安文物保护修复中心与美国西北大学学术技术部先进媒体制作室负责并具体实施完成。项目得到中国国家文物局、陕西省文物局和美国梅隆基金会的经费及物力支持，也得到西安市文物局和蓝田县文物部门的积极配合与支持。

3. 本书采用中文和英文，内容包括正文和图版两大部分。正文说明合作项目及应用技术的基本情况。图版采用的图像是从水陆庵项目高清晰的二维图像、虚拟漫游、三维模型、建筑横截面图、元数据和互联网界面等近800GB的数字图像资料中精选而出，以全视角的效果，反映了水陆庵及其彩绘泥塑群的历史、艺术、宗教和研究价值，也体现出数字化图像技术在文化遗产领域的应用前景。

4. 本书的出版得到中国国家文物局、陕西省文物局和美国梅隆基金会的支持，对此表示诚挚的谢意，同时也对支持本书出版的其他相关部门、单位、个人和项目组成员表示感谢。

Editor's Note

1. The compilation of this book has been based on the results of the Sino-American collaborative project "Applications of 3D scanning and digital image production technology at the Shuilu'an Temple in Lantian" and the publication of this work is also one of the outcomes of that project.

2. The Xi'an Center for the Conservation and Restoration of Cultural Relics and the Northwestern University Department of Academic Technologies (NUAMPS) were respon sible for the project and its implementation. The project received financial and material support from the State Administration of Cultural Heritage, the Shaanxi Provincial Bureau of Cultural Heritage, and the Andrew W. Mellon Foundation. It also received active cooperation and support from the Xi'an Municipal Bureau of Cultural Heritage and the antiquities authorities of Lantian County.

3. This work is published in both Chinese and English, and its contents are divided into text and illustrations. The text describes the basics of the collaboration and the technologies used. The pictures used for the illustrations have been carefully selected from almost 800Gb of digital data, and represent high-resolution 2D images, VR's, 3D models, architectural plans, metadata and Web interfaces.

4. The State Administration of Cultural Heritage, the Shaanxi Provincial Bureau of Cultural Heritage, and the Andrew W. Mellon Foundation have supported the publication of this work, and we extend to them our deepest appreciation. We would also like to thank all the other organizations, agencies, individuals and team members who have lent their support to the publication of this work.

目　录　TABLE OF CONTENTS

序　一

　　陕西蓝田古属京畿之地，文化遗产众多。考古发掘材料证明，距今约115万年的蓝田猿人，就在县境内公王岭一带繁衍生息。周安王二十三年（公元前379年）开始置县，以《周礼》玉之美者为蓝，县出美玉，故名蓝田。蓝田，玉山蓝水，风景秀丽，明代诗人刘玑有"天下名山此独奇，望中风景画中诗"之句，赞美蓝田山水之美。而水陆庵即坐落于这青山绿水之间，更兼有"小敦煌"之称的精美彩绘塑像群，令人流连。

　　作为遗产大国，中国政府一直致力于对文化遗产的保护，水陆庵一直受到陕西省政府的关注和保护。同时，陕西省文物管理机构十分注重采用现代科技手段保护古老的文明，注重与世界先进国家进行文化遗产的保护交流活动。陕西省文化遗产保护机构自20世纪80年代就开始与有关国家开展文化遗产保护交流活动，并卓有成效，许多国际友人因对陕西文化遗产保护工作的突出贡献，获得了中国政府和陕西省政府的赞誉和奖励。可以说，陕西文化遗产科技保护的蓬勃发展与国际有关遗产保护机构的帮助和支持是分不开的。

　　当今世界，科技与文化交融，数字文化遗产更是其中一个热点。中国西安文物保护修复中心与美国梅隆基金会、美国西北大学合作开展的《三维扫描及数字化图像制作技术在蓝田水陆庵的应用研究》正是采用这种现代技术来实施对文化遗产的保护和研究。中美双方采用高清晰度的数字技术和三维扫描技术对水陆庵精美的彩绘泥塑群进行了拍摄、测量，完成了全面储存翔实准确、多层次、多角度的水陆庵数字信息，为今后水陆庵泥塑的保护、研究、传播和交流以及其他遗产数字项目提供了技术、资料的基础。这项陕西文化遗产保护国际科技合作成果，受到陕西省政府赞赏和全国各界的关注，对陕西其他应用数字技术保护、保存文化遗产项目起到指导和典型示范的作用。

　　本书是中国西安文物保护修复中心与美国梅隆基金会和美国西北大学合作研究项目的介绍和总结。两国科技人员以一种新的方式保存、诠释中国悠久传统文化，使人们既可以感受历史遗产之美，也可以看到现代科技之奇。

　　即将搁笔之际，欣闻西安文物保护修复中心获批文物保护国际科技合作基地，这是对中心数年来文物保护国际科技合作成绩的一个肯定。望借此契机，中心更进一步，真正成为知名的国际化的文物保护机构。

　　是为序。

Preface I

Because of its location near many ancient capitals, Lantian in Shaanxi Province has an abundance of historical and cultural heritage. Archeological evidence has shown that as far back as 1.15 million years ago, the Lantian Ape Man lived and flourished in the vicinity of the Gongwang Hills within this county. A county was first established here in the 23rd year of King An of the Zhou Dynasty (379 BCE). According to the *Zhou Li (Rites of Zhou)*, blue jade was regarded as the most beautiful jade, and because beautiful jade was produced in this county, it was named "Lantian" ("Blue Jade.") With its jade-like mountains and blue rivers, Lantian's scenic beauty was praised by the Ming poet Liu Ji, who wrote that "Of all the famous mountains in the land, this is the most extraordinary, with scenery within the view and poetry within the painting." The Shuilu'an Temple is located amid these verdant hills and streams, and with the painted clay sculptures which have given it the nickname of "Little Dunhuang", it makes the visitor reluctant to leave.

As a country with a rich past, China's government has been consistently mindful of the conservation of its cultural heritage, and the Shaanxi provincial government has devoted attention and conservation efforts to the treasure that is the Shuilu'an Temple. At the same time, heritage conservation agencies in Shaanxi have placed great emphasis on using the techniques of modern science and technology to protect their ancient civilization, and they have stressed the need for exchanges in heritage preservation work with advanced countries around the world. Such exchanges began in the 1980's and have been highly productive. Many international friends have made outstanding contributions to heritage conservation work in Shaanxi, and have received recognition and awards from both the national and provincial governments. It is fair to say that the robust development of scientific conservation efforts in Shaanxi is inseparable from the assistance and support of international heritage conservation agencies.

At present, the integration of science and culture and the digitization of cultural heritage are particularly topical. The project on "Applications of 3D scanning and digital image production technology at the Shuilu'an Temple in Lantian" undertaken collaboratively by The Xi'an Center for the Conservation and Restoration of Cultural Relics, the Andrew W. Mellon Foundation and Northwestern University is precisely one which uses modern technology for heritage conservation and research. The Chinese and American teams utilized high resolution digital technology and 3D scanning to photograph and measure the painted clay sculptures of the Shuilu'an Temple. By comprehensively capturing accurate, multilevel and multi-perspective digital information from the Temple, they have provided a technical and informational foundation which can be used for future conservation, research, dissemination and exchange efforts at the Temple, as well as in other digital heritage projects. The outcomes of this international collaboration on scientific heritage conservation in Shaanxi have been favorably received by the Shaanxi provincial government and have been noted in other countries and circles. The project offers guidance and a model for other digital conservation and preservation efforts in Shaanxi.

Images of the Shuilu'an is both an introduction to and a summation of this collaborative project between The Xi'an Center for the Conservation and Restoration of Cultural Relics, the Andrew W. Mellon Foundation and Northwestern University. The technical specialists from both countries have found a new way to conserve and present China's ancient traditional culture. Through this work, the reader can appreciate both the beauty of the historical relics and the wonders of modern science and technology.

It gives me great pleasure to receive word that the Xi'an Center for the Conservation and Restoration of Cultural Relics has been designated a key center for international scientific and technological cooperation in heritage conservation. This is an affirmation of the Center's work in this area for the past several years, and I hope it will use this opportunity to make yet more progress and become a truly well known international institute of heritage conservation.

Liu Yunhui

序　二

　　本书是为推广科学技术、光大文化遗产这一普惠天下的共同事业，由众多远隔重洋、文化迥异、勤奋献身、才华横溢之团体齐心协力所获硕果的见证。此类成功合作是不同因素汇聚的成果，其结晶就是本项目的发展与完成。

　　第一个因素当首推水陆庵。这一独特建筑及其蕴藏的历史性艺术雕塑举世无双，与所有名副其实的伟大艺术一样令人叹为观止。笔者曾有幸在庵中工作，庵中之雕塑及其艺术魅力堪称永恒，今日观之与五年前首次观看时一样精美绝伦。

　　成功国际合作之第二个因素系有一支层层协力的全能团队。为本书效力的正是这样一支队伍，从斥资机构的资助，到书中所列主要参与团体，到陕西省当地各级支持，都为一个共同夙愿和目标同心奋斗。此项目的主要执行单位是中国西安文物保护修复中心和美国西北大学学术技术部，而敦煌研究院及我们的欧洲合作者林星格文化公司的参与充分反映了技术的全球化，显示这是个真正的 21 世纪项目。

　　此次成功合作之第三个因素是专心投入的工作人员。没有他们，这项工作是不能完成的。美方项目经理斯特芳妮·佛斯特不厌其烦地协调在美国的工作，同时也监督现场的图像采集；拉尔斯·胡布里克则负责与我们欧洲合作者的联系与制作。

　　美国前总统西奥多·罗斯福说："生活所能赋予之最佳奖赏莫过于为值得献身之事业艰苦奋斗之机会。"本书就是这样一项事业，这样一项多方合作、艰苦奋斗、值得献身的事业。

哈伦·瓦拉克（万里）

Preface Ⅱ

This book is an example of the good that can come from the collaboration of geographically distant and culturally disparate, yet dedicated and talented groups working for a common beneficial cause for the development, and distribution of technology and cultural heritage. A successful collaboration such as is this is the result of many pieces existing and coming together in one specific time and place. All of the pieces came together in the development, and completion of this project.

The Shuilu'an Temple is, of course, the first piece. The unique building, and the historical and artistic sculptural treasures that exist within it are one of kind in the world. It falls in to the realm of the incomprehensible, like all truly great artistic works. After having had the privilege to have worked in the temple I can say that the sculpture and the physical effect of the art in the Temple does not diminish over time, it remains as startling and beautiful on the seeing it now as it did when first introduced it over five years ago.

The second piece of a successful international collaboration is that there must be a comprehensive team that exists and functions together at all levels. This project had such a team, from the support of the funding organizations, the principal participating institutions listed in this book, to the support at all levels in Shaanxi Province. The principal implementers of this project were the Xi'an Center for Conservation and Restoration of Cultural Relics and Northwestern University, but the involvement of the Dunhuang Academy and our European partner, Linsinger Kultur, fully demonstrates the globalization of technology and shows it to be a truly 21ˢᵗ century endeavor.

The third piece of this successful collaboration was the dedicated staff without whom it would never have been completed. Stefani Foster, the U.S. project manager worked tirelessly managing the domestic production as well as overseeing the on site photo acquisition, and Lars Hubrich managed the communication and production done with our European partner.

To quote an American president, Theodore Roosevelt, "Far and away the best prize that life offers is the chance to work hard at work worth doing." Surely this was such a project, one that many groups had to collaborate and work hard, and one that was surely worth doing.

Harlan Wallach

水陆庵与彩绘泥塑群

　　蓝田水陆庵位于中国陕西蓝田县城以东10公里的普化镇王顺山下，距西安约60公里。蓝田水陆庵以琳琅满目的彩色泥塑著称于世，为陕西年代最久、规模最大、保存最完整的佛教雕塑群，具有极高的历史、艺术和研究价值，有着"小敦煌"之美誉，现为中国国家级重点文物保护单位。

　　蓝田水陆庵南依巍峨秦岭，北临涛涛灞河。蓝水出悟真峪后，一分为二，将水陆庵环绕成一个天然的鱼形小岛。据《蓝田县志》记载，水陆庵为悟真寺的"蓝诸庵水陆殿"。悟真寺创建于隋开皇年间（公元581～604年），宋重修多宝塔碑文载："山中有寺乃是隋朝兴建，唐时扩建，命尉迟敬德监修。"悟真寺是佛教净土宗的发祥地，是一座著名的皇家寺院，净土宗的名僧善导大师和净业大师曾在此开坛讲经。其后，法成、慧远、慧超等净土宗的高僧先后皆较长时间居住于此。悟真寺僧人重多，殿宇鳞次，规模扩展到悟真峪的南普陀和北普陀地区，"蓝诸庵水陆殿"

水陆庵鸟瞰图　　Bird's-eye view of Shuilu'an

就建在北普陀。到了明代，秦潘王朱怀埢于嘉靖四十二年至隆庆元年（公元1563～1567年），动用能工巧匠，大兴土木修缮庙宇，精雕细绘重整壁塑，历时五年竣工。朱怀埢的母亲经常到这里烧香拜佛，把水陆殿奉为家祀佛堂。悟真寺的"蓝诸庵水陆殿"，现名"水陆庵"可能与此有关。古往今来，历朝历代都对水陆庵进行了维修和保护，古朴清幽的寺院与参天郁葱的翠柏交相辉映，使之成为游览观光的胜地。白居易、王维、杜甫等许多文人墨客都在这里留下了诗篇。

　　现在的蓝田水陆庵坐西向东，占地面积6800平方米，有诸圣水陆殿五间、耳房两间、中殿三间、前殿五间，大殿至前殿之间南北各有厢房十三间，总建筑面积约1600平方米。1988年，又新修仿明歇山顶山门三间。水陆庵彩色泥塑集中于水陆殿内，殿外悬挂有中国佛教协会会长、著名书法家赵朴初题写的匾额。在这座面积不大的殿堂内，中国古代的雕塑工匠以卓越的智慧，在十三个墙面上精确合理地安排和塑造了三千余尊彩色泥塑。这些诸佛人物、亭台楼阁、山水湖海、珍禽异兽分布在大殿的角角落落，令人目不暇接。众多的彩色泥塑布局巧妙，大小各异，错落有致，不仅内容丰富，场面宏大，人物众多，而且佛教主题突出，层次分明。其以中隔墙的"横三世佛"造像为中心向四周辐射，对面东前檐墙西壁分别安排报身佛卢舍那和应身佛释迦牟尼造像。三世佛的背面雕塑有观世音、文殊、普贤菩萨，南、北梢间横墙上置药王菩萨和地藏菩萨五大菩萨造像。在三世佛两侧的南、北山墙上安排有佛本生、佛本行和佛经变等佛传故事的连环壁塑、悬塑。其中北山墙是以佛降生故事为中心，正中塑有释迦牟尼"托胎"、"降生"、"九龙浴"，而南山墙是以佛"涅槃"为中心，正中塑有"涅槃"的场景和人物。同时，南北山墙上还塑有相互连贯、气势磅礴、场面宏大的"五百罗汉过海"和"二十四诸天"等。在整个西檐墙的东壁布局着"佛升仞利天为母摩耶夫人说法"佛传故事巨幅彩塑群。在水陆殿里，佛教中的主要人物和佛传故事位置突出，形象显著，并且前后左右遥相呼应，陪衬烘托。水陆庵彩塑体现了我国古代雕塑巧妙多变的塑造技艺和强烈的艺术震憾力，既突出了佛教的思想内容，也反映了当时的社会生活。

　　唐代是中国佛教的兴盛时期，其佛教雕塑借鉴吸收了中外的雕塑和绘画技巧，创造了许多具有民族特色的佛教艺术作品。到了明代，蓝田水陆庵佛教雕塑艺术在继承中国佛教艺术传统的基础上，造像群和壁画的艺术风格更加趋向写实，增添了世俗生活的色彩。在蓝田水陆庵的彩色泥塑群上，雕塑匠师们在保留了唐代佛教雕塑技法的同时，充分发挥了泥塑的工艺技巧和绘画手法。从大到五六米高的主佛或菩萨，小到四五厘米的比丘或乐伎，无论是骨架、胎体和雕塑手法，还是造型、神态、色彩、服饰，都体现出了中国泥塑灵活多样的雕塑技艺特点，圆雕、浮雕、镂空等技法展现得淋漓尽致。这些艺术大师们雕塑的诸佛、菩萨，形体丰满，神态逼真；阿难、迦叶睿智温顺，老诚稳重；天王和护法力士凶猛威武，忠心不二；佛传故事中的连环壁塑、悬塑，人物鲜活，情节生动。同时，佛座、背光、亭台楼阁、古刹宝塔装饰繁缛富丽，凝重辉煌；珍禽瑞兽、鱼鸟花草更是惟妙惟肖，栩栩如生。水陆庵中泥塑表面敷以金箔，施红、黄、绿、青、紫、蓝、白等无机矿物颜料，展示出了中国古代彩绘精湛的水平，形象生动逼真，质感细腻，色彩丰富。这些都在中国的艺术史上留下了光辉一页。

　　蓝田水陆庵的彩色泥塑群是中国佛教艺术的代表佳作之一，为研究中国宗教历史、建筑、雕塑、工艺、音乐和民俗等提供了重要的资料，是古代劳动人民留给世界的珍贵文化遗产。历年来，其都得到了中国政府的重视和保护，也得到国际文化遗产保护机构的帮助和支持。

The Shuilu'an and its painted clay sculptures

The Shuilu'an is located at the foot of the Wangshun Mountains in Puhua Township, 10 km. east of the county seat of Lantian in Shaanxi Province. It is approximately 60 km. from Xi'an. The temple is renowned for its dazzling clay sculptures, which are the oldest, largest and best preserved group of Buddhist sculptures in Shaanxi Province. They are a rare treasure and part of China's outstanding cultural heritage, with great historical, artistic and scholarly value. The temple has the lovely nickname of "Little Dunhuang," and is a nationally protected key heritage site.

The Shuilu'an is situated by the majestic Qin Mountains to the south and the rushing Ba River to the north. After passing through the Wuzhen Valley, the Lan River divides in two, forming the natural fish-shaped island on which the temple is located. According to the Lantian County Gazetteer, the Shuilu'an was once the Shuilu Pavilion within the Lanchu Nunnery of the Wuzhen Temple. The Wuzhen Temple was originally built during the Kaihuang reign of the Sui dynasty (581 ~ 604 CE). When its Duobao Pagoda was rebuilt in the Song dynasty, the stele inscription noted that "the temple in these mountains was built during the Sui and expanded during the Tang. Chi Jingde was ordered to oversee its rebuilding". The Wuzhen Temple was a famous imperial temple where the Pure Land sect of Buddhism flourished. The famous monks Master Shandao and Master Jingye both taught sutras there, and subsequently learned monks of the Pure Land sect including Facheng, Huiyuan, and Huichao lived at the temple for extended periods. The Wuzhen Temple had many monks and numerous buildings, and expanded all the way to the south Putuo and north Putuo districts of the Wuzhen Valley. The Shuilu Pavilion of the Lanchu Nunnery was built in north Putuo. From the 42nd year of Jiajing to the first year of Longqing during the Ming dynasty (1563 ~ 1567 CE), Zhu Huaijuan, Prince of Qin, employed skilled artisans and craftsmen in a major five-year reconstruction which involved exquisite painting and carving. Zhu Huaijuan's mother often came here to offer incense to Buddha, and adopted the Shuilu Pavilion as her family temple. The renaming of the Shuilu Pavilion of the Lanchu Nunnery as the Shuilu'an Temple may have been related to this episode. Over the years and generations, the Shuilu'an Temple has been oft-repaired and maintained. Its plain and ancient buildings are set off by verdant towering pine trees, just as its natural beauty and deep-rooted religious culture enhance each other. Hence, the Shuilu'an Temple has naturally become both an attraction for visitors in search of scenic beauty and a place of worship for the religiously devout. Many famous writers of old, including Bai Juyi, Wang Wei and Du Fu, have their travel records and poems here.

The present-day Shuilu'an Temple lies west and faces east, and occupies a total area of 6,800 sq. m. The five-bay Shuilu Pavilion houses the religious figures and has two side wings; there is a middle pavilion with three bays, and a front pavilion with five bays. There are thirteen side chambers each lining the north and south sides between the main pavilion and the front pavilion, and a total floor space of approximately 1,600 sq. m. In 1988, a new Ming style front gateway with three openings was added. The clay sculptures of the Shuilu'an Temple are located within the Shuilu Pavilion, above which hangs a horizontal plaque inscribed with the words "Shuilu'an" written by the renowned calligrapher Zhao Puchu, President of the Chinese Buddhist Association. Inside, along the thirteen wall surfaces within this pavilion of modest size, are arranged some three thousand painted freestanding, wall and hanging clay sculptures, as well as wall paintings. These were crafted by ancient Chinese artisans with great ingenuity, using superb traditional folk art decorative techniques and a variety of artistic methods. The many Buddhist figures, buildings and balconies, landscapes and oceans, and unusual animals are arranged over every nook and cranny of the pavilion and dazzle the eye. The numerous sculptures are cleverly laid out, vary in size and orderly in their seeming randomness. They have a wealth of content, a massiveness of scale and a profusion of characters; moreover, the Buddhist themes are particularly evident and the sculptures very clearly layered. They are centered around the "Horizontal Buddhas of Three Manifestations" at the dividing wall in the middle and project out from there. Opposite this group, along the North Wall East of the front chamber, are statues of Locana Buddha and Śākyamuni. Five Bodhisattvas are represented: statues of three -Avalokiteśvara, Mañjuśrī and Samantabhadra-are behind the Buddhas of Three Ages, and Bhaisajya-rāja and Kṣitigarbha are positioned along the South Wall West and North Wall West of the front chamber. On both sides of the Buddhas of Three Manifestations, on the North and South Walls of the front chamber, stories about Buddha from the Jātaka Tales, Buddhacarita Tales and Buddhist sutras are told through sequences of wall sculptures and hanging sculptures. The main theme of the North Wall is Buddha's birth, and at its center are scenes of "Buddha's entry into his mother's womb," "Buddha's birth" and "The nine-dragon bath." The main theme of the South Wall is Parinirvāna, and at its center is a scene of Parinirvāna and various characters. The North and South Walls also feature a massive, interlinked and magnificent depiction of "The Five Hundred Arhats Crossing the Sea" and a group of large statues of the Twenty Four Divine Guardians. The entire West Wall is filled with an enormous sculpture group portraying the tale of "Buddha ascending Trāyastrimśas to preach to Queen Māyā." Also depicted are leaders of the three religions of Buddhism, Daoism and Confucianism, ten famous physicians, kings and generals, merchants and farmers, representing contents from Chinese folk religion. Inside the Shuilu Pavilion, these major Buddhist figures and stories are prominently placed, clearly delineated, matched and balanced. These complex yet delicate and colorful sculptures typify the ingenious and variegated design and spectacular artistry of traditional Chinese sculpture. They highlight Buddhist religious concepts while at the same time conforming to folk traditions.

Buddhism reached its zenith in China during the Tang dynasty, hence it was during the Tang that Buddhist sculpture absorbed and assimilated the best sculptural and painting techniques from China and abroad to create many Buddhist artworks with Chinese characteristics. By the Ming dynasty, and building on a foundation of Chinese traditional Buddhist art, the artistry of the Buddhist sculptures from the Shuilu'an Temple in Lantian had added national, secular and drawn-from-life features which were based on changes and developments in social life, ideas and religion, resulting in the sculptures and frescoes having a more realistic artistic style. In creating the painted clay sculptures and frescoes of the Shuilu'an, the artisans retained the carving techniques of Tang Buddhist sculptures, while at the same time fully utilizing their skills in sculpting clay and in painting. Sculptures -as large as the 5～6 m. tall main Buddhas and Bodhisattvas and as small as the 4～5 cm. tall monks and musicians - exhibit in their lines, surfaces and carving, in their shapes, appearance, colors and garments the freedom of extension and sculptural liberty which is typical of Chinese clay sculpting. Techniques such as carving in the round, relief work and hollow work are fully utilized. The Buddhas and Bodhisattvas created by these master craftsmen have full-fleshed bodies, realistic appearances and harmonious proportions. Kāśyapa and Ānanda are wise and gentle, honest and steady; the Divine Guardians and guardians are fierce and loyal. In the sequences of wall sculptures depicting tales about Buddha, the characters are lifelike and the story lines vivid. At the same time, the thrones, auras, buildings, balconies and pagodas are sumptuous and ornate, imposing and magnificent. The riding animals, mythological birds and beasts, flora and fauna are perfectly rendered and almost lifelike. The multicolored clay sculptures exemplify the virtuosity of traditional Chinese painting. The main color comes from gold leaf, to which inorganic red, yellow, green, aqua, purple, blue and white pigments are applied. This gives the statues, garments and scenery a realistic appearance, subtle texture and rich tones. They are a bright chapter in the history of Chinese art.

The painted clay sculptures at the Shuilu'an Temple in Lantian are a representative masterpiece of late Chinese Buddhist art. They offer important materials for the study of China's religious history, architecture, sculpture, crafts, music and folkways, and are a precious cultural heritage bequeathed to the world by workers and master craftsmen of ancient times. Over the years, the Chinese government has given them attention and conservation efforts, and they have also attracted assistance and support from international cultural heritage conservation organizations.

水陆庵彩绘泥塑群数字影像项目概况

（一）项目背景

蓝田水陆庵彩色泥塑群规模大，数量多，体态大小各异，布局错落有致，雕塑工艺精湛，色彩丰富，涉及题材内容广泛，彩绘和制作工艺亦非常特殊，保存了多种古代文化和艺术的信息，具有极高的历史、艺术和研究价值，是中国古代重要的文化遗产和稀世珍宝。由于水陆庵的泥塑是用泥土等材料制作，并插、悬在泥墙上，泥像历经千年，严重的风化侵蚀、屋面渗漏、土墙空臌等自然灾害时时刻刻威胁着文物的安全，现已有部分塑像脱落、颜色褪变，面临着保护和永久保存的困难。中国各级政府对水陆庵彩色泥塑群的保护高度重视，逐步采取了科学有效的保护措施和加固技术。但是，蓝田水陆庵彩色泥塑群没有系统、完整的数字信息资料，使保护和管理工作受到一定的影响。在"数字遗产"工程已成为文物工作的重点之一的当今，采用高清晰度的数字技术和三维扫描技术拍摄、测量水陆庵立体彩色泥塑群的多层次、多内容、全方位的图像是非常紧迫的任务，储存翔实准确、全面完整的彩色泥塑和文物病害的数字信息资料是非常必要和重要的工作。这种数字资料信息对彩色泥塑群类文化遗产的管理、保护、研究、利用将起到非常重要的作用。

2003年初，中国西安文物保护修复中心与美国西北大学经过考察和磋商以后，向美国梅隆基金会推荐了《三维扫描及数字化图像制作技术在蓝田水陆庵的应用研究》项目。随后，梅隆基金会与西安文物保护修复中心签署"中美合作的蓝田水陆庵数字图像项目"协议。该项目经过中国国家文物局批准，由中国陕西省文物局领导，中国西安文物保护修复中心与美国西北大学学术技术部先进媒体制作室负责具体实施，中国国家文物局、陕西省文物局以及美国梅隆基金会分别对项目的开展给予了财力和物力的支持。合作项目得到了西安市文物局、蓝田县文物旅游局和水陆庵文管所的积极配合与支持。2003年2月至2007年5月期间，经过中美双方专业技术人员的通力合作，精心工作，项目圆满结束，取得了显著的成果，并通过了中美专家委员会的评审和陕西省文物局的验收。

（二）项目组织

1. 项目批准

   中国国家文物局

2. 项目监督和领导

   中国陕西省文物局

3. 项目支持

   中国西安市文物局、蓝田县文物旅游局、水陆庵文物管理所

4. 合作单位

   中国西安文物保护修复中心、安德鲁·W·梅隆基金会

5. 执行单位

中国西安文物保护修复中心、美国西北大学学术技术部

（三）项目目的

通过对蓝田水陆庵彩色泥塑进行全方位的数字化图像信息的项目，为此达到：

＊协助中方培养二维、三维图像、VR 漫游的专业技术人员；

＊运用计算机技术对蓝田水陆庵泥塑进行高清晰度数字化图像存储和使用（宣传、研究、保护修复、出版）；

＊美国梅隆基金会把蓝田水陆庵彩色壁塑的图像纳入 ARTstor 数字图书馆，允许其用户为非商业性的教育、文化和慈善项目的学术、研究和教育使用；

＊中国西安文物保护修复中心成为 ARTstor 数字图书馆水陆庵彩色壁塑图像的用户成员；

＊提供在世界范围宣传和展示蓝田水陆庵彩色壁塑艺术的途径，促进文化交流、科学研究、文物保护修复、文物旅游等；

＊通过开发新浏览和注释工具及使用本项目所产生的多类型数据，以探讨学术应用互联网的潜力。

（四）项目成果知识产权

中方独家拥有由基金会和（或）其指定代表制作的本项目的数字化图像的知识产权，其中包括在中心工作人员和学员协助下制作的数字化图像。中方对水陆庵图像的所有权将包括以其选择的任何方式使用水陆庵图像，包括用于商业和非商业目的。但不限于用传统媒体和在互联网上的发表权、署名权、修改权、保护权、复制权、改编权、分发权、展览权、广播权、以表演再现权、展示权、制片权和演绎权。

（五）项目进程

2003 年，项目前期调研和实地考察，合作意向确定。

2004 年，蓝田水陆庵彩色泥塑群局部尝试性二维拍摄及处理。

2005 年，项目获得国家文物局批准。中美双方签定正式合作协议，进行了蓝田水陆庵水陆殿及泥塑的二维、三维数据现场采集。

2006 年，蓝田水陆庵水陆殿及泥塑的二维、三维数据后期制作，元数据整理和输入，以及开展数字信息应用研究。

2007 年，在西安召开了项目的总结汇报、验收评审会议，中美专家组成评审委员会对项目作出了评审结论。

2009 年，项目主要成果编辑出版。

Digitization of the painted clay sculptures at the Shuilu'an

I. Background of the Project

The painted clay sculptures of the Shuilu'an are vast in scale, large in number, diverse in form, intricate in layout, skillfully sculpted, and rich in color. Many types of historic, cultural and artistic information have been preserved in their impressive content and composition and in their extraordinary painting and craftsmanship. They are extremely valuable for research in history and art, and are an exquisite part of China's ancient cultural heritage. Over a span of almost a thousand years, because the painted clay sculptures were carved out of materials such as clay and stuck onto or suspended from earthen walls, their existence has been seriously threatened by natural forces such as wind erosion, leakages from the roof, and bulging of the hollow earthen walls. Some sculptures have fallen off, and colors have changed. They are confronted by difficulties in their conservation and permanent preservation. Various levels of governments in China have devoted a great deal of attention to the conservation of these sculptures at Shuilu'an, and methodically employed scientific and effective measures to protect and reinforce them. However, the lack of systematic and complete digital information about them has to some degree hampered the work of conserving and managing them. Today, as the "Digital Heritage" project has become a key part of work on cultural relics, there is a pressing need to use high resolution digital technology and 3D scanning technology to photograph and measure the full extent of the sculptures from every angle and every level. The compilation of accurate and complete digital information on the sculptures and the damage they have sustained is an essential and important task. Such work will allow the information to play an important role in the management, conservation, study and usage of the sculptures.

For these reasons, in early 2003, after site surveys and consultations with Northwestern University, the Xi'an Center for the Conservation and Restoration of Cultural Relics suggested the project "Applications of 3D scanning and digital image production technology at the Shuilu'an Temple in Lantian" to the Andrew W. Mellon Foundation. Subsequently, the Foundation and the Center signed an agreement for a "Sino-American Collaborative Project on Digital Imaging of the Shuilu'an Temple." This project was approved by the State Administration of Cultural Heritage, overseen by the Shaanxi Province Bureau of Cultural Relics, and implemented by The Xi'an Center for the Conservation and Restoration of Cultural Relics and the Northwestern University Department of Academic Technologies (NUAMPS). Financial and material support was given to this project by the State Administration of Cultural Heritage, the Shaanxi Provincial Bureau of Cultural Relics and the Andrew W. Mellon Foundation. The project received the active cooperation of and support from the Xi'an Municipal Department of Cultural Relics, the Lantian County Department of Cultural Relics and Tourism, and the Shuilu'an Office of Cultural Relics Management. Chinese and American specialists worked together closely from February 2003 until May 2007, and through their meticulous efforts, the project came to a fruitful conclusion and yielded outstanding results which were evaluated by Chinese and American experts and accepted by the Shaanxi Provincial Bureau of Cultural Relics.

II. Organization of the project

1. Project Approvals:

State Administration of Cultural Heritage

2. Project Oversight and Guidance：

Shaanxi Provincial Bureau of Cultural Relics

3. Project Supporters:

Xi'an Municipal Department of Cultural Relics, Lantian County Department of Cultural Relics and Tourism, Shuilu'an Office of Cultural Relics Management

4. Collaborating Organizations:

Xi'an Center for the Conservation and Restoration of Cultural Relics, Andrew W. Mellon Foundation

5. Implementing Organizations:

Xi'an Center for the Conservation and Restoration of Cultural Relics, Northwestern University Department of Academic Technologies (NUAMPS)

III. Project Goals

To undertake a comprehensive digitization of the clay sculptures at the Shuilu'an Temple in Lantian in order to:

* assist the Chinese side in training technical specialists in the production of 2D and 3D images and VR's;

* use computer technologies to store and utilize (publicize, study, conserve and repair, publish) the high resolution digital images of the sculptures;

* enable the Andrew W. Mellon Foundation to place the images in the ARTstor Digital Library to allow their use for scholarly, research and educational purposes in noncommercial educational, cultural and philanthropic work;

* allow the Xi'an Center for the Conservation and Restoration of Cultural Relics to become a user of the ARTstor images of the Shuilu'an clay sculptures;

* provide a channel through which the art of the Shuilu'an sculptures can be disseminated and displayed globally, thereby promoting cultural exchanges, scientific studies, conservation and restoration of the relics, cultural tourism, etc.

* explore the potential of the Internet for scholarly applications through the development of new browsing and notation tools and the use of the many types of data generated by this project.

IV. Intellectual Property Rights of the Project Results

The Chinese side holds the exclusive intellectual property ownership rights in the digital images created for this Project by the Foundation, and/or its designated representatives, including those images created with the assistance of the staff and trainees of the Center. The Chinese side has the right to use the Shuilu'an images in any manner it chooses, including for commercial and non-commercial purposes. The ownership rights of the Chinese side with respect to the Shuilu'an images include, but are not limited to, the rights to publish, attribute, modify, protect, reproduce, adapt, distribute, exhibit, broadcast, to reproduce through performances, display, film, and extrapolate the Shuilu'an images in both traditional media and the Internet.

V. Progression of the Project

2003: preliminary site visit and confirmation of intentions.

2004: trial photography and image postproduction of a portion of the Shuilu'an sculptures.

2005: project approval received form the State Administration of Cultural Heritage. Chinese and American sides sign formal agreements of collaboration. On-site data collection of 2D and 3D date conducted on the Shuilu Pavilion and the sculptures within.

2006: postproduction of 2D and 3D data of the images. Metadata input. Study initiated on applications of the digital data.

2007: conference in Xi'an for presentation and acceptance of results. Evaluation committee of Chinese and American experts offer assessment of project.

2009: editing and publication of major project outcomes.

水陆庵彩绘泥塑群数字影像项目
应用技术及影像成果

随着科技的进步和数字化技术不断发展,在不断加强对文物本体保存现状、风化机理和加固技术等诸多方面研究的同时,数字遗产工作已成为当前文物保护工作的重点之一。2005 年至 2007 年间,中国西安文物保护修复中心与美国西北大学学术技术部进行了《三维扫描及数字化图像制作技术在蓝田水陆庵的应用研究》项目,经过努力,在物质文化遗产的数字化采集、处理、储存、共享技术的应用上取得了显著的成果。

蓝田水陆庵古代木构建筑的特殊结构和布局,使其内部存世的彩色泥塑群的二维及三维高清晰、高分辨率图像的采集存在不少的难点,导致这些珍贵的文物至今没有整体或局部的高清晰图像资料。针对蓝田水陆庵这种大面积、大景深的立体泥塑群,项目对图像采集和后期计算机处理等技术问题进行了深入的研究,采取了多种数字图像技术,完成了对其全方位的数字化图像采集和处理。项目主要研究和应用了四种数字化图像技术,即二维高清晰数字摄影与制作、虚拟漫游拍摄与制作、古建筑的三维测量测绘及建模、三维扫描与制作技术。水陆庵泥塑十三个墙面的二维高清晰数字图像的拼接和元数据的添加链接,实现了 Internet 上的对大幅面图像的浏览,累计处理数据量约 390G,形成的水陆庵泥塑各壁面图像 2×13 = 26G,清晰度可达到 1 毫米可见;水陆殿的七个图像采集点的虚拟漫游的制作,实现了水陆殿泥塑的仿真游览;水陆殿数字建模,并辅以数字摄影贴图,达到水陆殿三维场景再现,并可通过水陆殿三维模型,精确获取大量的测量测绘数据;水陆殿北山墙泥塑三维扫描的拟合、矫正及贴图等处理,形成了北山墙泥塑的三维立体图像,精度达到了 0.1 毫米,实现了泥塑 360 度的全方位的旋转展示。在此基础上,对水陆庵泥塑的所有文字、图像数据资料进行的整合,使建筑及泥塑历史背景、塑造内容、二维图像、虚拟漫游、三维模型、研究论著等各方位的泥塑资料均能在 Internet 平台上展示,通过数字化技术全视角的诠释水陆庵泥塑,实现数据资料共享交流。

物质性文化遗产是不可再生的。数字化图像技术为全面保存这些文化遗产的信息资料提供了有力手段。通过本项目的研究和实践,解决了大型的、不可移动文化遗产对技术实施和处理的难题,全面实现了翔实准确的多层次、多内容文化遗产数字化信息资料的采集、处理、储存和共享,对文化遗产的管理、保护、研究、交流等具有重要指导和借鉴意义。

(一)二维高清晰数字摄影

中国古代建筑,尤其木构建筑的特殊结构和布局,使其内部存世的泥塑、壁画的二维平面图像拍摄存在不少的难点,如光的使用、幅面大小、体态各异等,以至这些珍贵的文物没有整体的和局部的高清晰图像资料。数字摄影技术的发展打破了传统摄影的种种局限,特别是在计算机软件这个"暗房"的帮助下,使许多传统相机和暗房难以驾御的拍摄方法得以轻易实现。

水陆庵彩色泥塑群的合成图像，是由高像素数码摄影机拍摄的一系列二维图像组成的，这个过程包括两个基本的步骤，即现场拍摄工作和后期制作。

现场拍摄是能够得到清晰准确的图像的基础工作，拍摄效果的好坏，直接影响后期制作以及整体图像的保真度。由于水陆庵彩色泥塑群布局和结构的特殊性，图像的拍摄不同以往的平面拍摄，如拍摄壁画，而是一个立体的拍摄，需要保证整体的清晰度，十分复杂。拍摄图像前要进行认真的勘察和设计，制定能使每个壁面的整体和局部都能被采集到的周密的拍摄方案，并在整个拍摄过程中严格遵循执行。构成的合成图像的每个单幅图像都要按大型栅格规划图的排列进行拍摄，数码相机的机位与被采集壁面正交，并与所采集的壁面始终保持等距离，而且机位必须在轨道和机架上绝对水平、垂直的等距离移动。每次平行、垂直拍摄的每张照片与前一张照片必须有50%的覆盖率。这种方法使我们能够从同一个角度以极高的清晰度拍摄壁面的每张照片，包括边界和角落。当然，为了绝对保证文物的安全和达到高清晰图像的技术指标，焦距和光线也有严格的要求和拍摄技巧。拍摄中，除了主摄影师以外，其他人员有明确的分工，如灯光、场记、机位移动等都要各负其责。

水陆庵数字化图像工作产出了海量的数据文件，拍摄全部的彩绘泥塑总面积有300多平方米，塑像3700余尊，共拍摄数码照片1420余幅，每幅照片4096×5456（2200万）像素，原始数据达130GB。这些数据对文物保护和研究非常珍贵。数据管理和工作是由专职数据管理员监督。拍摄开始前，他协助制定摄影的栅格尺寸和方案。在采集图像过程中，他把图像转移到计算机，并对每个单幅图像的质量和元数据进行严格检查。之后，他要为数据文件的归类、编码、分发和传输进行备份和储存。

后期制作是对专业和技巧的挑战。在后期制作过程中，所采集的二维图像数据被拼接组合成完整的泥塑群壁面和立体的大型泥塑照片，使原彩色泥塑群作为一个统一、完整、逼真的整体图像再现。拼接过程主要使用Photoshop把各个壁面原来重叠分拍的全部单幅图像拼接成一幅完美并能显示每个雕塑细节的合成图像。这个工作实际上是对专业人士素质和技巧的考验，在这个过程中有许多技术难点需要克服，如色差、变形等诸多的问题。拼接后的图像的效果是令人满意的，所显示的壁面有些细节是现场所看不到的，特别是现场观察的盲区和极精微的细节也能清楚看到，所有的雕塑、壁塑、悬塑一目了然。

（二）虚拟现实摄影

虚拟漫游（Virtual Reality）是通过由计算机硬件、软件及各种传感器构成三维信息的人工环境——虚拟环境。这种虚拟环境是使用者在视、听、触、嗅等感知行为处于虚拟三维的逼真体验中。通常在文物领域主要使用的是三维全景虚拟现实（也称实景虚拟）。这种技术是在数字摄影技术的基础上，使用特殊的拍摄器材和专门的计算机软件得以实现。

根据水陆庵水陆殿建筑和泥塑群的布局，在水陆庵的虚拟漫游图像的拍摄时，选择了七个图像采集点，共拍摄数码照片268幅，每幅照片4992×3320（1600万）像素，原始数据达18GB。通过营造良好的自然光照效果和各个机位、角度的数字摄影，制作的360度泥塑群的虚拟漫游，使参观、浏览及研究有身临其境的感觉，做到了参观路线与泥塑内容的统一。

VR采集的初步是以摄影机的光学中点为中心而进行的一系列360度环绕单幅拍摄。所获取的静态照片与相邻两张有约25%的覆盖率，静态照片装入图像VR处理软件后，这些图像的重复部分会被自动对接和拼接，处理后成为一幅连续的全景影片。

每个VR影片由一系列360度环绕拍摄组成（每环分6张拍摄），其中包括水平拍摄、仰拍（30～60度间）和俯拍（负30～60度间），另有90度仰拍和负90度俯拍各一张。然后利用上述不同角度拍摄的图像，制作出含有水平线和垂直线360度视线的球形全景。

由于VR是通过一个点来观看一个空间，所以每个采集点的机位选点是非常重要的。效果最好的全景需要使用最广角的镜头来拍摄，因此，为了获取足够的细节，摄影机的位置必须靠近全景的主要焦点。在决定水陆殿内全景的数量和采集点的位置时，摄影师既要注意到适合用VR表现的彩塑细节，也要注意到水陆殿的整体布局和空间感，这才能使一系列影片准确地、无缝地描绘整个现场。

RealViz Stitcher是用来拼接及制作QTVR影片的软件。VR专家把重叠的图像对好，然后软件通过识别重叠或相同界线对图像进行自动拼接。不过，这个过程通常出现误差。当全景已经拼成而"揭开"为TIF文件后，VR专家必须使用部分信源文件来修补TIF文件，纠正软件所产生的（如倍增或线条不连续）的误差，专家另要接入曝光正确而不含有摄影机或三角架的图像和门口和地面图像。纠正误差后，VR专家再把TIF文件"打包"成MOV文件格式，最后观看的是完整及经过纠正的QTVR。

最后，使用Pano2VR软件来把基于TIF的VR全境转化为基于Flash的VR影片，以便于学术数据库和浏览工具界面易于使用操作。

（三）建筑测绘

测绘学是技术性科学，它的形成和发展在很大程度上依赖测量方法和仪器工具的创新和改革，近二十年来，科学技术的新成就，计算机技术、微电子技术、空间技术等新技术的发展和应用，传统测绘技术向数字化测绘技术转化。3D技术、GPS、GIS、CAD、近景摄影以及三维激光扫描仪等技术和设备已得到广泛的使用。

本项目的三维测量测绘使用了多种测绘技术手段，综合应用，如采用全站仪对实体的几何空间进行定点，使用激光测量测绘技术，获取各个点的三维空间坐标，使用数字建模软件形成三维模型，并结合摄影测量技术，获取了诸如墙面、屋顶等全部的三维空间数据，再辅以数字摄影贴图，达到实体三维场景再现，使水陆殿的三维模型更加真实可靠。

文物遗迹或考古遗迹的数字化成果，大多是按照不同媒介的特征而不是按照原址的结构来展示的。本项目尝试在网上界面来展示古建筑文物水陆殿的数字图像，特别是表现古建筑文物与实际现场的相互关系。为此，建立了虚拟现场的坐标系统。中心点坐标是相对于水陆殿模型的坐标原点（0，0，0），以公尺为单位，显示该点距原点的x、y、z平面的距离。数字文物的范围是中心点与各个平面的实际距离，而坐标则界定范围的中心。这些空间元数据用以建立水陆殿三维模型和平面图的空间浏览界面供用户使用。

（四）三维扫描

三维扫描就是测量有形物体表面的三维坐标数据，而每一个数据（点）都带有相应的x、y、z坐标数值，这些数据（点）集合起来形成的点云（Point Cloud），就能构成物体表面的特征。它是通过三维激光扫描仪或者三坐标测量仪对物体表面进行三维的扫描或测量，获得物体的三维点云数据，再利用逆向工程软件对获得的三维扫描数据进行整理、编辑、获取所需的三维特征曲线，最终通过三维曲面表达出物体的外形。随着三维扫描技术的发展，其扫描精度已能达到毫米乃至微米级。

高精度的三维扫描技术应用到像水陆庵这样大面积、大数量、分布错落的立体彩色泥塑群上，在世界上目前可能属于首次。无论是现场的扫描数据收集，还是后期制作处理，都是一个大数据量、拼合精细、极具挑战性的数字化图像的科研攻关课题，是一次有意义的尝试。

三维模型和现场测量的采集和初步的后期处理工作是委托奥地利林星格文化公司完成的。主要对蓝田水陆庵水陆殿北山墙部分彩塑群进行了三维扫描，扫描面积20多平方米，扫描次数2324次，原始数据达27GB，其中一尊天王像扫描的精度为0.1毫米，其他部分扫描的精度为0.4毫米；为了后期制作彩塑群三维图像能达到色彩的还原，图像的逼真，对扫描的区域拍摄了数码照片1093幅，每幅照片4992×3320（1600万）像素，原始数据达68GB。制成完成了十二尊泥塑和六幅局部壁塑的三维图像模型。

三维模型建立主要是经过现场数据扫描采集，后期合成以及色彩处理等过程完成的。这是一项复杂程度和技巧难度极高的工作，是对智力和体力的考验，在此难以述及。另外，水陆庵彩绘泥塑壁面的线条和塑像与土墙的结合十分复杂，往往有个别地方因扫描不到而缺少点云数据。这些缺口也需要后期解决。

完成后的三维模型以 VRML 文件格式输出，通过 3D Studio 软件压缩转化，使其可以在互联网上传送。最后，模型再转化成 Director Shockwave 软件格式，通过网上插件，使用者可以自由操纵每个三维模型。

（五）基于互联网的数据整合及共享

当今，互联网已经成为全球信息共享的主要途径。文物的特殊性决定了文物"数字化"必然会产生海量的信息。如何通过互联网，使人们能够便利地访问各类文物信息成为文物数字化利用和文物信息传播的瓶颈。对此，本项目通过对形成的海量水陆庵数字化信息：建筑及泥塑历史背景、塑造内容、二维图像、虚拟漫游、三维模型、研究论著等数字资料进行整合，使其能够在基于互联网的使用平台上达到共享，同时追求各方位的水陆庵泥塑资料不受时间和空间限制服务于大众，从而可对文物的管理、研究、保护、交流、教育等产生积极的推进作用。

数字水陆庵的各类信息提供两种层面共享：

对于专业研究者，可通过基于互联网的高清晰图像元数据录入工具，来浏览研究高清晰图像，也可以为不同内容的图像添加塑像特征的解释、翻译、状况及修补资料等注释。注释区可由用户调整，并可小到细节、大到整体，以达到最广泛的文物研究者全面的对图像进行元数据的添加及整理。

高清晰图像元数据录入工具是以Flash/Actionscript 2应用软件插入Plone内容管理系统软件而操作的。Plone系统软件可使分散在不同地方的研究者容易地共享所录入的元数据。该系统可提供共享、全文搜索及RSS布告通知改变等。

对于普通用户，可通过基于互联网的学术数据库和浏览工具，全面浏览水陆庵彩色泥塑的高清晰图像、全景虚拟现实电影、可漫游的三维模型、建筑黄截面图和文字及技术元数据等资料。

为了保存原物的现场环境，以及在观看文物展示的同时，保留文物现有的物质关系。每件文物的网页都具有其相关的二维高清图像、三维模型及VR全景，并且在该网页上能够显示文物及技术元数据及与其有关联的相关资料。这些链接都以缩略图的形式展示，可以点击链接到相关文物的网页等等。

学术数据库和浏览工具是利用Zope 3网络应用软件通过附加在Flash和Director/Shockwave客户软件上实现的。在浏览工具中，普通用户还可以利用图像放大器来浏览高清晰图像。

The technologies applied to the digitization of the painted clay sculptures and their outcomes at the Shuilu'an

With the steady progress of science and digital technology, "digitizing heritage" has become one of the focal points of present-day work in heritage preservation, along with research on improving the conservation of actual relics, studies on wind erosion mechanisms and techniques for reinforcement. In 2005 ~ 2007, the Xi'an Center for the Conservation and Restoration of Cultural Relics and Northwestern University Information Technologies Department of Academic & Research Technologies (NUAMPS) undertook the project "Applications of 3D scanning and digital image production technology at the Shuilu'an Temple in Lantian," and this effort yielded notable results in the digital capture, processing, storage and sharing of physical heritage objects.

The distinctive structure and layout of Shuilu'an's wooden building presents considerable difficulties for the creation of 2D and 3D high resolution images of the extant painted clay sculptures housed therein, and to date there have been no high resolution images of them in part or in whole. Given the large coverage area and great depth of field of the standing clay sculptures there, the project required in-depth study of the necessary image capture and postproduction computer technologies, and by utilizing a variety of digital imaging technologies, comprehensive digital image capture and processing was achieved. This project primarily studied and used four technologies, namely 2D high resolution digital photography and processing, VR photography and processing, 3D surveying, measuring and modeling of the building, and 3D scanning and production. High resolution 2D images were created of all the painted clay sculptures along the 13 wall surfaces within Shuilu'an and then stitched together; metadata was added and linked; and these resulted in large images which can be browsed over the Internet. Approximately 390 Gb of data was processed, yielding $2 \times 13 = 26$Gb of 1 mm resolution images of sculptures along entire walls.

The VR's produced from images captured at seven nodes offer realistic navigation around the sculptures in the Shuilu Pavilion. The digital model of the Pavilion, augmented with mapped digital photographs, is a 3D recreation of the building, and a large volume of survey and measurement data can be derived from the 3D model. Through contour matching, correcting and texture mapping of scans, a 3D model of 0.1 mm resolution was created of the statues along the North Wall which enables them to be rotated and displayed 360 degrees. All available textual information on Shuilu'an and its image data was integrated with this foundation, so that it is possible to display online all forms of information on the sculptures, including the history of the building and sculptures, the contents of the sculptures, 2D images, VR's, 3D models and research articles. As the sculptures are digitally represented from all perspectives, data is shared and exchanged.

Physical cultural heritage cannot be regenerated, and digital imaging technology offers an effective means of conserving information and data on such heritage. Through the research and implementation of this project, the technical difficulties of working on a large, immovable heritage site were resolved, and the accurate capture, processing, storage and distribution of digital data from a multilayered and complex heritage site was achieved. This has great significance for the management, conservation, study and exchange of cultural heritage.

I. 2D High resolution digital images

Traditional Chinese architecture, and particularly the distinctive structure and layout of this wooden building, presents many challenges for the 2D photography of interior clay sculptures and frescoes, for instance in lighting and framing, and in the varying sizes of the subjects. Hence, there are no extant high resolution records of these treasures either in part or as a whole. The development of digital photography techniques has broken through many of the limitations of traditional photography, especially in its use of computer software as a "darkroom" to readily accomplish what traditional cameras and darkrooms cannot.

The composite images of the Shuilu'an clay sculptures are formed from a series of 2D images photographed with high-pixel digital cameras. There are two basic parts to this process, namely on-site photography and postproduction.

On-site photography is the basis for creating clear and accurate images. The quality of the photography directly affects the fidelity of postproduction and the entire composite image. Because of the distinctive composition and layout of the Shuilu'an clay sculptures, the photography here differed from that usually used for flat surfaces such as frescoes. To shoot three-dimensional objects while ensuring the clarity of the whole is an extremely complex undertaking. Prior to shooting, thorough surveying and designing were required in order to produce a detailed work plan which allowed the entirety and each part of every wall to be captured, and this plan had to be strictly adhered to. All the individual photographs which went into the composite were photographed in a large grid layout. The digital camera was positioned perpendicularly to each surface being captured and was always at the same distance from the surface. Camera movements along the rails had to be at equal intervals and absolutely horizontal and vertical. Each shot had to overlap the adjacent horizontal and vertical shots by 50%. Use of this method allowed the taking of extremely high resolution photographs even at edges and corners. Of course in order to ensure the safety of the relics and to meet demanding technical specifications, there were also high demands on focus, lighting and photographic skills. During the course of shooting, apart from the chief photographer, other team members also had clear job assignments, including lighting, note-taking and camera positioning.

The digital imaging of Shuilu'an created a vast amount of data. The roughly 3,700 sculptures photographed covered an area of approximately 300 sq.m. A total of 1,420 photographs were taken, each one 4096×5456 (22 million) pixels in size, yielding 130 Gb of raw data. This data is invaluable for the conservation and study of the relics. Data management and handling was overseen by a data management specialist. Prior to each shoot, he assisted in designing the measurements of the shooting grid; during the shoot, he transferred the images to a computer and rigorously inspected each individual image for quality and metadata; subsequently, he had to back up and store the data files for classification, numbering, distribution and transmission.

Postproduction is a challenge to both expertise and skill. During this process, the captured 2D digital images were stitched together into complete photographs of sculpture groups and large freestanding clay statues in such a way that they were reproduced as a unified, complete and realistic whole. Photoshop was used for most of the stitching, in which the overlapping portions of the individual images were stitched into a complete composite where every detail of each sculpture was visible. This was a test of the caliber and skill of the technical staff due to the many technical difficulties such as color differences and geometric distortions which had to be surmounted in this process. The stitched composite images are gratifying to look at, as they reveal some details which cannot be seen on site. In particular, blind spots and extremely fine details can be clearly observed, and all the freestanding statues, wall sculptures and hanging sculptures are visible at a glance.

II. Virtual Reality images (VR's)

Virtual Reality is an artificial environment--a virtual environment -- created with three dimensional information from computer hardware, software and various sensory transmission devices. Such virtual environments cause the user to have a realistic experience through use of the senses, such as vision, hearing, touch or smell. In work related to cultural objects, the primary type of virtual reality used is three-dimensional virtual panoramic reality (virtual scenes.) This technique is based on a foundation of digital photography, and is implemented through the use of special photographic apparatus and computer software.

Taking into account the layout of the Shuilu Pavilion building and the clay sculptures within it, seven nodes were selected as image capture points for the shooting of the Shuilu'an VR's. A total of 268 photographs were taken, each one 4992×3320 (16 million) pixels, yielding 18 Gb of raw data. Through the creation of good naturalistic lighting effects and digital photography from a variety of camera locations and angles, the 360° VR's of the clay sculptures impart a "you-are-there" sensation of visiting, browsing and studying, and achieve a unity between the route of travel and the content of the sculptures.

The first step of VR capture is the shooting of a complete 360° circle of photographs from the optical center of the camera. Each of these still pictures overlaps approximately 25% with the adjacent ones, and after they are loaded into the VR software, the redundant portions of the images are excised and the pictures stitched together into a continuous panoramic film.

Each of the VR's films is composed of a 360° circle of photographs (six pictures to a circle), and the films include one taken horizontally level, one at an upward tilt (30 ~ 60°), one at a downward tilt (− 30 ~ 60°), and single shots upward at 90° and downward at − 90°. These images taken at different angles are then used to produce a spherical panorama with a 360° field of vision both horizontally and vertically.

Because a VR observes a space from a single point, the location of each node is extremely important. The highest quality panoramas must be photographed with extreme wide-angle lenses; hence, in order to capture a sufficient amount of detail, the camera must be placed near the most important parts of the panorama. In deciding on the number of panoramas and node locations inside the Shuilu Pavilion, the photographers had to take into consideration both how the VR would display the details of the sculptures and also the overall layout of the Pavilion and its spatial feel. Only by doing so can the series of films accurately and seamlessly represent the entire site.

RealViz Stitcher was the software used to stitch and produce the QTVR's. VR specialists matched the overlapping images, which were then automatically stitched together by the software through recognition of redundancies or shared boundaries. However, errors often appear during this process. Once the panorama is stitched and "unfolded" into a .TIF file, the VR specialists must use some source files to repair the .TIF files and correct the errors introduced by the software (such as doubling or broken lines). They must also insert correctly exposed images which do not show the camera or tripod, as well as images of the doors and floor. After the errors are corrected, the VR specialists "package" the .TIF files into .MOV files, and the product which is ultimately viewed is a complete and corrected QTVR.

Finally, Pano2 VR software is used to convert the panoramic .TIF VR files into Flash VR films, which provide a user-friendly interface for scholarly databases and browsing tools.

Ⅲ. Architectural Surveying

Surveying is a technical science, the emergence and development of which has, to a large extent, relied on innovations and improvements in survey methods and instruments. In the past two decades, new scientific achievements including the development and applications of computer technology, microelectronics and spatial technologies have caused traditional surveying techniques to move toward digital surveying. 3D technologies, GPS, GIS, CAD, close-up photography and 3D laser scanning techniques and equipment are now all being used extensively in surveying.

The 3D surveying in this project employed a varied of survey methods in an integrated manner. For example, a total station was used to determine the location of objects in geometric spaces; laser scanning survey techniques were used to determine the coordinates of various points in three-dimensional space; mathematical modeling software was used to create three-dimensional models. These were combined with photogrammetry to obtain all the three-dimensional data of the walls, roof, etc. and then digital photographs were mapped to the models, resulting in three-dimensional re-creation of objects and producing a more realistic and reliable three-dimensional model of the Shuilu Pavilion.

Most results from the digitizing of cultural objects or archeological sites are displayed according to the characteristics of various media rather than the structure of the original. This project attempts to display digital images of the ancient Shuilu Pavilion through an online interface, and in particular to show the relationships between the building and the objects at the site. A virtual coordinate system was set up for this purpose. The central coordinates correspond to the original coordinates of the Shuilu Pavilion model (0, 0, 0). Distances from this point are indicated along the x, y and z planes in meters. The boundaries of a digital relic are the actual distances from its center to all three planes, and the coordinates define the center point of the boundaries. The 3D model of the Shuilu Pavilion and the building plans generated by this spatial metadata are made available to users through a spatial browser.

IV. 3D Scanning

A 3D scan measures the three-dimensional coordinates of the surfaces of a material object, and each piece (point) of data includes corresponding values for the x, y and z coordinates. Together this data (points) from a point cloud captures the features of the object's surfaces. The 3D point cloud data is obtained through 3D scanning or measuring, either with a 3D laser scanner or with equipment which measures the three coordinates. The point cloud is then sorted and edited with reverse engineering software to yield the necessary 3D contours, and finally the 3D contours are used to show the external shape of the object. With the development of 3D scanning technology, scans of a millimeter or finer are now possible.

The use of high-precision 3D laser scanning on sculptures as large in area, as numerous, and as irregularly arranged as those at Shuilu'an may have been the first attempt of this sort in the world. Both the on-site data collection and the postproduction work involved large volumes of data and precise matching. As an extremely challenging effort in digital imaging, this endeavor had special significance.

Both the initial data collection for 3D modeling and on-site surveying and the postproduction work was entrusted to the Austrian firm Linsinger Kultur. The bulk of the 3D scanning was done on a portion of the clay sculptures along the North Wall of the front chamber of Shuilu'an. The area scanned was some 20 sq. m. large, and it required 2,324 scans to produce 27 Gb of raw data. One of the Divine Guardians was scanned at a resolution of 0.1mm, while the rest were scanned at 0.4mm. To ensure color accuracy in postproduction and realism of the final images, 1,093 digital photographs were taken of the scanned area, each 4992×3320 (16 million) pixels in size, for a total of 68 Gb of raw data. 3D models were completed of twelve Divine Guardians and six sections of the wall sculptures.

The creation of a 3D model is done primarily through the on-site collection of scanning data, its postproduction synthesizing, and color management. This extremely complex and difficult work is both physically and intellectually challenging, but cannot be described in detail here. Moreover, the Shuilu'an clay sculptures, wall contours and joints between walls and sculptures are very intricate, so point cloud data is lacking for some spots where scanning was impossible. These lacunae also had to be resolved during postproduction.

The completed 3D models were exported as VRML files and compressed and converted with 3D Studio software to enable their transmission over the Internet. Lastly, the models were converted again into Director Shockwave files so that with the help of an online plug-in, users can freely manipulate each 3D model.

Ⅴ. Web-based Data Integration and Sharing

At present, the Internet has become the main channel for global information sharing. Because of the unique characteristics of cultural objects, their "digitization" inevitably generates enormous quantities of information. The bottleneck in the use and transmission of information from cultural objects lies in the problem of how to allow users to conveniently access various types of information online. In this project, the tremendous volume of information generated about the Shuilu'an Temple--the historical background of the building and sculptures, the contents of the sculptures, 2D images, VR's, 3D models and research articles--had to be integrated and organized so that they could be shared across an Internet-based platform. Another goal was to allow users to access the Shuilu'an materials at any time and from any location, so as to facilitate their use for management, research, conservation, exchanges and education in the field of cultural relics.

The various types of digital information from Shuilu'an can be accessed at two levels:

For specialists and scholars, they can be accessed through an online metadata entry tool for the high resolution images. The images can be browsed and studied, and explanations, interpretations, descriptions and other notes on the features of the sculptures can be added. In addition, the annotation zone can be varied in size by the user, and can range from a small detail to the entirety. This allows the broadest range of cultural heritage researchers to add metadata to and help organize the images.

The metadata entry tool for the high resolution images is a Flash/Actionscript 2 application software operated through a Plone content management system software plug-in. Plone system software allows users at different locations to readily share the metadata they have entered. This system offers sharing, full-text searches and RSS notifications.

For ordinary users, access is available through an online scholarly database and browser through which they can browse the high resolution images of the sculptures, VR's, navigable 3D models, section plans of the building, text and metadata.

To preserve the environment of the site and to retain the material relationships of the cultural objects as they displayed, the Web page for each object includes all its related 2D high resolution images, 3D models and VR's. The same Web page can also display object and technical metadata and other related materials. These links are displayed as thumbnails which can be clicked to bring the user to the corresponding pages.

The scholarly database and browser are based on Zope 3 Web application software and implemented with a Flash plug-in and Director/Shockwave client software. The browsing tool also offers ordinary users the capability to zoom in as they browse the high resolution images.

图　版
PLATES

壹　二维高清晰数字摄影

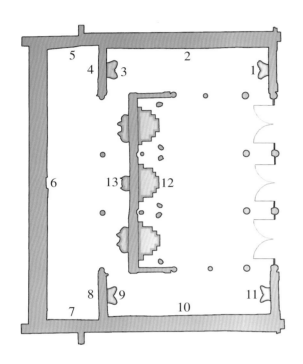

水陆殿泥塑分布图。水陆庵的彩绘泥塑分布在水陆殿内，总计有十三面墙壁，面积400多平方米，共三千余尊彩绘泥塑。

Placement of clay sculptures inside the Shuilu Pavilion: the painted clay sculptures of Shuilu'an are housed in the Shuilu Pavilion along thirteen vertical surfaces. There are approximately 3,000 painted clay sculptures covering over 400 sq. m.

中国古代建筑，尤其木构建筑的特殊结构和布局，使其内部存世的泥塑、壁画的二维平面图像拍摄存在不少的难点，如光的使用、幅面大小、体态各异等，以至这些珍贵的文物没有整体的和局部的高清晰图像资料。数字摄影技术的发展打破了传统摄影的种种局限，尤其在计算机软件这个"暗房"的帮助下，使许多传统相机和暗房难以驾御的拍摄方法得以轻易实现。

水陆庵彩色泥塑群的合成图像，是由高像素数码摄影机拍摄的一系列二维图像组成的，这个过程包括两个基本的步骤，即现场拍摄工作和后期制作。

水陆庵数字化图像工作产出了海量的数据文件，拍摄全部的彩绘泥塑总面积300多平方米，塑像3700余尊，共拍摄数码照片1420余幅，每幅照片4096×5456（2200万）像素，原始数据达130GB。这些数据对文物保护和研究非常珍贵。

Ⅰ. 2D High resolution digital images

Traditional Chinese architecture, and particularly the distinctive structure and layout of this wooden building, presents many challenges for the 2D photography of interior clay sculptures and frescoes, for instance in lighting and framing, and in the varying sizes of the subjects. Hence, there are no extant high resolution records of these treasures either in part or as a whole. The development of digital photography techniques has broken through many of the limitations of traditional photography, especially in its use of computer software as a "darkroom" to readily accomplish what traditional cameras and darkrooms cannot.

The composite images of the Shuilu'an clay sculptures are formed from a series of 2D images photographed with high-pixel digital cameras. There are two basic parts to this process, namely on-site photography and postproduction.

The digital imaging of Shuilu'an created a vast amount of data. The roughly 3,700 sculptures photographed covered an area of approximately 300 sq.m. A total of 1,420 photographs were taken, each one 4096×5456 (22 million) pixels in size, yielding 130 Gb of raw data. This data is invaluable for the conservation and study of the relics.

1　**东前檐墙北梢间西壁**

North Wall East, Front Chamber

高：4.3 米，宽：3.2 米，9 张单副照片

H：4.3m，W：3.2m，9 photographs

　　这部分彩绘泥塑主佛报身佛卢舍那居中，下坐莲台，上擎幡盖，后有背光，身旁左右各塑立一侍者。其周围分三层，由下至上，第一、二层塑有护法金刚力士，站立云头，有的手持法器，有的抱拳合掌，第三层幡盖周围有供养人、双头飞天及动物等。主佛上方塑有释、道、儒三教领袖，均坐云头之上。中为佛教释迦牟尼；北为儒教孔丘，左手持有管乐器；南为道教李耳，左手持磨杵，右手持有竹简，上有灵芝。

　　The main Buddha figure in this group of painted clay sculptures is Locana Buddha , seated on a lotus throne with a patākā shade overhead, a painted halo to the rear, and an attendant on each side. The area surrounding the main statue is arranged in three horizontal tiers. From bottom to top: the first and second tiers feature guardian figures, some standing on clouds, some holding ritual objects and others with their palms together. On the third tier, attendants, doubled-headed devas and animals surround the patākā shade. Above the main statue are leaders of the three main religions (Buddhism, Daoism and Confucianism), sitting in a row atop the clouds. Śākyamuni sits in the middle, with Confucius to the north, holding a musical instrument in his left hand, and Laozi to the south, holding a pestle in his left hand and a bamboo slip in his right.

E - 3

CF000527

E - 2

CF000526

E - 1

CF000523 　　　　　CF000524

D

CF000521

C

CF000519

B

CF000513

A - 2

CF000510

A - 1

CF000511

2 报身佛卢舍那、三教领袖
Locana Buddha (the Cosmological Buddha), three religious leaders

3 孔丘
Confucius

4 释迦牟尼、双头飞天
Śākyamuni, Two-headed devas
5 李耳
Laozi
6 护法金刚
Guardians

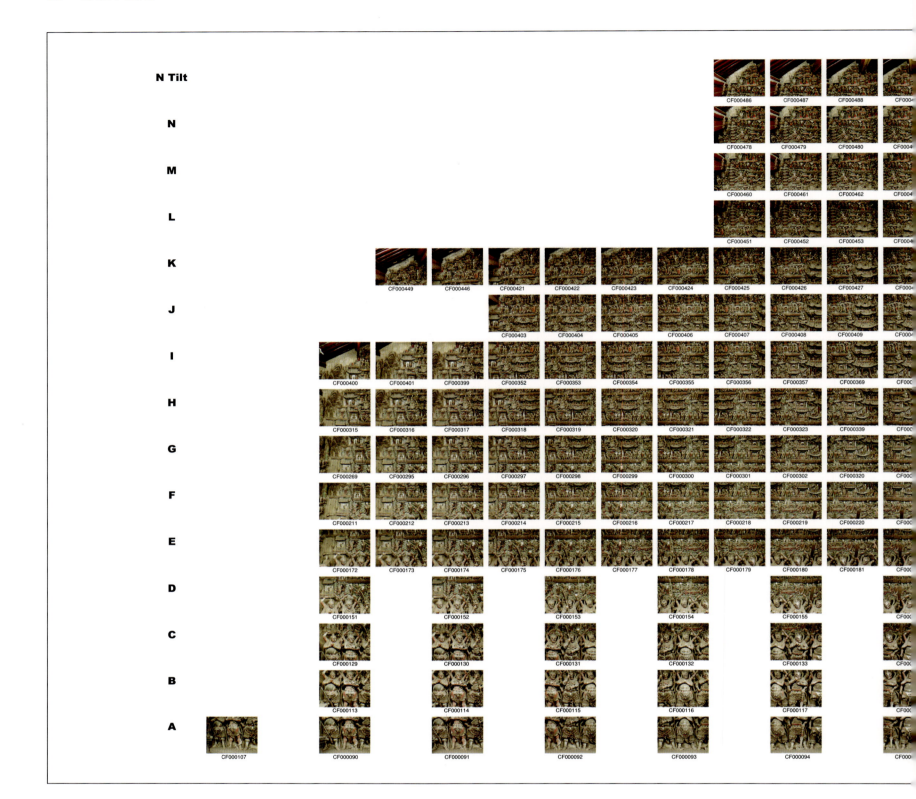

7 北山墙东南壁

North Wall, Front Chamber

高：7.4米，宽：11.0米，238张单幅照片

H：7.4m，W：11.0m，238 photographs

  这部分彩绘泥塑由下至上，第一层二十四诸神，也有称为天龙八部，塑有十二尊，与南山墙合为二十四尊。这组塑像有的两头两臂，有的三头六臂，有的四头八臂，有的手持利刃，高举法器，有的足踩怪物。第二层塑五百罗汉过海，塑有罗汉二十五尊，与南山墙合为一整体。此面的塑像以大海为背景，有的乘船，有的踏浪，有的骑鱼虾鳖怪，在北山墙西还有龙王携众欢迎的场景。在壁塑中，有的罗汉从山上，有的从河流中，有的从寺院中，有的从路上，都正集结加入渡海的行列中。第二层到最上层之间的正中三重庑殿内，主要塑有"释迦八相"佛本行故事。"托胎"：在三重庑殿上方，有一个乘六牙白象的菩萨，从天而降。殿内，塑有躺在床上的摩耶夫人，有六牙白象抚摸她的右腋，于是摩耶夫人便怀了胎。"出胎"：在三重庑殿第二层的左角，塑立着摩耶夫人举着右手，侍者从她的右腋下抱起才出生的悉达多太子。"九龙浴"：在三重庑殿内，塑有一个妇人抱着悉达多，上有九龙吐水为他沐浴。"降生"：在三重庑殿正中央，塑有金色的悉达多太子左手指天，右手指地，作狮子吼。以庑殿为核心，还辐射有佛本生故事连环壁塑，如"割肉贸鸽"、"舍身饲虎"等等。最上层是诸佛说法的场景。

000490 CF000491 CF000492 CF000493

000482 CF000483 CF000484 CF000485

000464 CF000466 CF000467 CF000468

000455 CF000456 CF000457 CF000458

000429 CF000430 CF000431 CF000439 CF000440 CF000441 CF000442 CF000443 CF000444 CF000447 CF000448

000411 CF000412 CF000413 CF000414 CF000415 CF000416 CF000417 CF000418

000360 CF000361 CF000362 CF000363 CF000370 CF000365 CF000366 CF000367 CF000368 CF000396 CF000397 CF000391

000326 CF000327 CF000340 CF000329 CF000330 CF000331 CF000332 CF000333 CF000334 CF000335 CF000336 CF000337 CF000338

000305 CF000308 CF000283 CF000285 CF000286 CF000287 CF000288 CF000289 CF000290 CF000291 CF000292 CF000293 CF000294

000222 CF000223 CF000224 CF000225 CF000226 CF000227 CF000228 CF000229 CF000230 CF000231 CF000232 CF000233

000183 CF000184 CF000186 CF000187 CF000188 CF000189 CF000190 CF000191 CF000192 CF000193 CF000194 CF000195

CF000157 CF000159 CF000160 CF000161 CF000162 CF000163

CF000135 CF000136 CF000138 CF000139 CF000140 CF000141 CF000113

CF000119 CF000120 CF000122 CF000123 CF000124 CF000125 CF000126

CF000096 CF000098 CF000099 CF000100 CF000101 CF000102 CF000103

From bottom to top: the first tier contains the twenty-four Divine Guardians also known as the Eight Classes of Beings. There are twelve statues on this side and twelve more along the South Wall. Some statues are two-armed and two-headed, some six-armed and three-headed, and some eight-armed and four-headed. Some are holding sharp weapons, some are raising ritual objects aloft, and others are trampling on monsters. The second tier depicts the Five Hundred Arhats Crossing the Sea. The twenty-five arhat statues on this side form a complete whole together with those along the South Wall. In the background behind the statues is the sea, with some arhats riding on boats, some walking on the waves and others mounted on strange sea creatures . The west side of the North Wall also features a scene of the Dragon King leading crowds in welcoming the arhats,. Among the wall sculptures there are arhats converging from mountains, rivers, temples and roads, all en route to join the sea voyage. In the central section between the second tier and the topmost tier is a three-story building with a hip roof, where the eight aspects of the Buddha's life as told in the Jātaka Tales are depicted. "Entry into the mother's womb": above the building, a bodhisattva riding a 6-tusked white elephant descends from the skies. Inside, there is a sculpture of Queen Māyā lying on the bed. The elephant caresses her right armpit, resulting in her pregnancy. "Birth": in the left corner of the building's second story, Queen Māyā stands with her right arm raised while attendants lift the newborn Prince Siddhārtha out of her right armpit. "The nine-dragon bath": inside the building, a woman holds Prince Siddhārtha while nine overhead dragons spew water for the infant's bath. "Descent into the world": at the center of the building, a gold-colored Prince Siddhārtha points to the sky with his left hand and to the earth with his right, while roaring like a lion. With the building at the center of the composition, other Jātaka Tales, such as the Śibi Jātaka and Tiger Jātaka, are depicted in sequential sculptures. The top tier shows scenes of various preaching Buddhas.

8 十二尊神将、罗汉过海、降生、
佛本行故事、佛本生故事
**12 Divine Guardians, Arhats Crossing
the Sea, Descent into the world,
Buddhacarita Tales, Jātaka Tales**

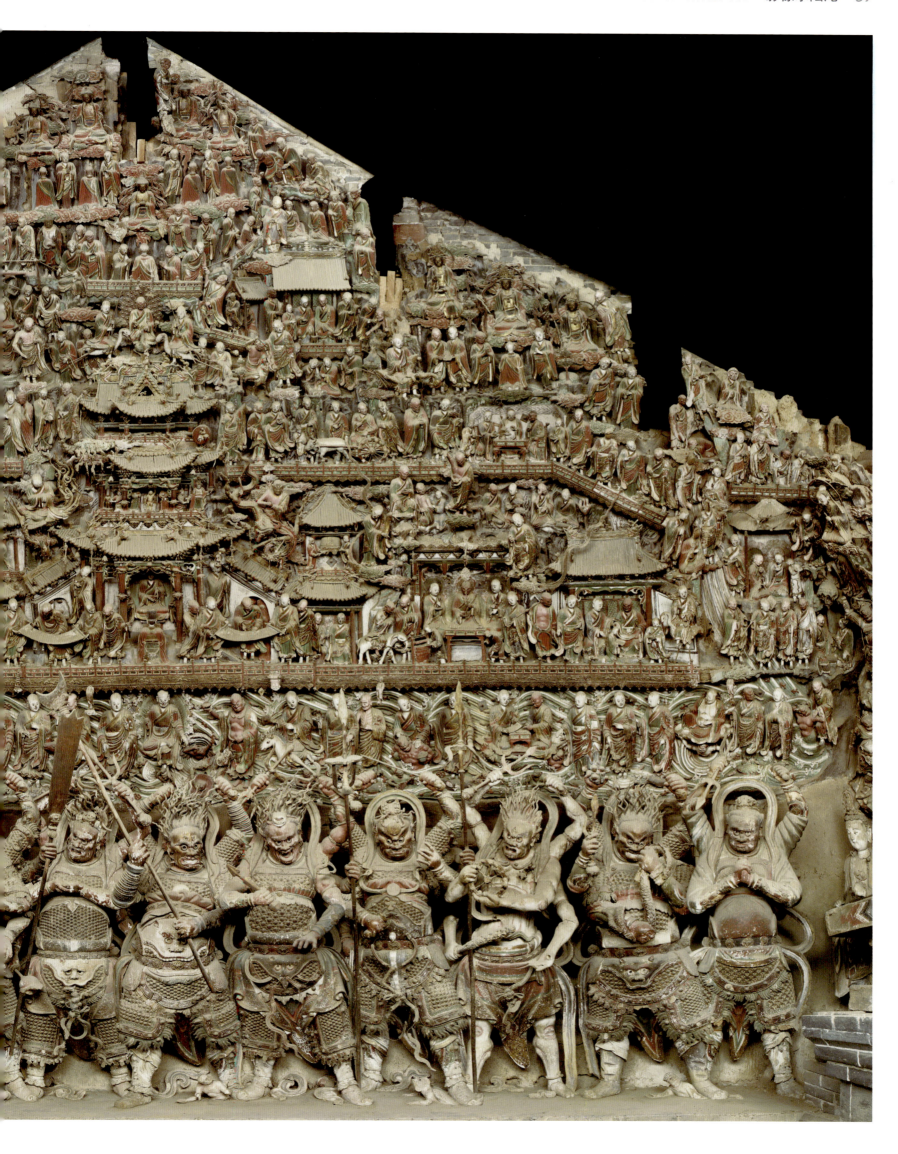

9 十二尊神将、罗汉过海 12 Divine Guardians, Arhats Crossing the Sea

10 十二尊神将（局部）
12 Divine Guardians (Partial)

11 十二尊神将（局部）
12 Divine Guardians (Partial)

12 十二尊神将（局部）
12 Divine Guardians (Partial)

13 十二尊神将（局部）
12 Divine Guardians (Partial)

14 十二尊神将（局部）
12 Divine Guardians (Partial)

15 十二尊神将（局部）
12 Divine Guardians (Partial)

16 北山墙东南壁（局部）
North Wall, Front Chamber (Partial)

17 北山墙东南壁（局部）
North Wall, Front Chamber (Partial)

18 北山墙东南壁（局部）
North Wall, Front Chamber (Partial)

19 阿私陀仙人
The holy man Asita

20　托胎、出胎、九龙浴、降生（朝天吼）
Entry into the mother's womb, Birth, The nine-dragon bath, Descent into the world (roaring at the skies)

21　孔雀明王
The Peacock King

22 乘龙罗汉
Arhat astride a dragon

23　驾凤罗汉
Arhat Riding on Phoenix

24 钟楼
Bell tower

25　鼓楼
Drum tower

26 舍身饲虎、割肉贸鸽
Tiger Jātaka, Śibi Jātaka

E - 3

CF000557 　　CF000558

E - 2

CF000556

E - 1

CF000555

D

CF000552 　　CF000551

C

CF000549

B

CF000544

A

CF000536

27 北梢间横墙东壁

North Wall West, Front Chamber

高：4.3米，宽：3.2米，9张单幅照片

H：4.3m，W：3.2m，9 photographs

这部分彩绘泥塑主佛地藏菩萨居中，下坐莲台，后有背光，左右各立一侍者。周围分三层，塑有供养人立于云朵上，头部残损。

　　The main statue is Ksitigarbha seated on a lotus throne, with a halo behind him and flanked by an attendant on each side. The adjacent area is divided into 3 horizontal tiers featuring sculptures of attendants standing atop clouds. The heads have been damaged.

28 地藏菩萨、闵公、道明和尚
Ksitigarbha, Lord Min, Daoming the monk
29 地藏菩萨（局部）
Ksitigarbha Detail (Partial)

30　供养人

Attendants

31 闵公
Lord Min

D

CF001871 CF001872 CF001873 CF001875 CF001874

C

CF001853 CF001854 CF001856 CF001857

B

CF001844 CF001845 CF001846

A

CF001830 CF001831 CF001832

32 北梢间横墙西壁

North East Wall, Rear Chamber

高：4.3米，宽：3.2米，27张单幅照片

H：4.3m，W：3.2m，27 photographs

这部分彩绘泥塑主佛十六臂十六眼观音菩萨居中，也称如意轮王菩萨。菩萨下坐莲台、波浪，上方左右两手持日轮、月轮，背有背光、竹园。其周围亭台楼阁林立，间有小型泥塑，为观音变故事。

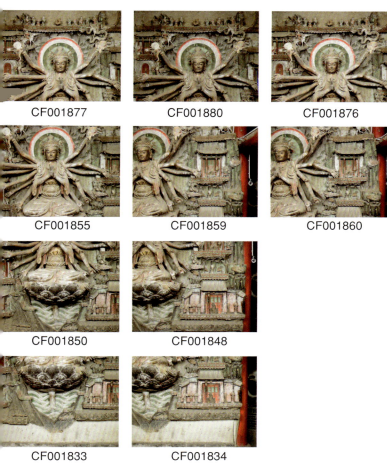

CF001877 CF001880 CF001876 CF001881 CF001882

CF001855 CF001859 CF001860

CF001850 CF001848

CF001833 CF001834

The main statue in this section is a sixteen-armed sixteen-eyed Avalokiteśvara, or possibly the Bodhisattva with a Talismanic Wheel. He is seated on a lotus throne atop the waves, with the sun and the moon in his left and right hands respectively. There is a halo and bamboo garden behind the statue. The many surrounding balconies and pavilions with small scale clay figures illustrate tales from the Avalokiteśvara Sutra.

33 十六臂十六眼观音菩萨（如意轮王菩萨）
Sixteen-armed Sixteen-eyed Avalokiteśvara (the Bodhisattva with a Talismanic Wheel)

34　观音变、日轮、月轮
Avalokiteśvara Sutra Tale, Sun disc, Moon disc

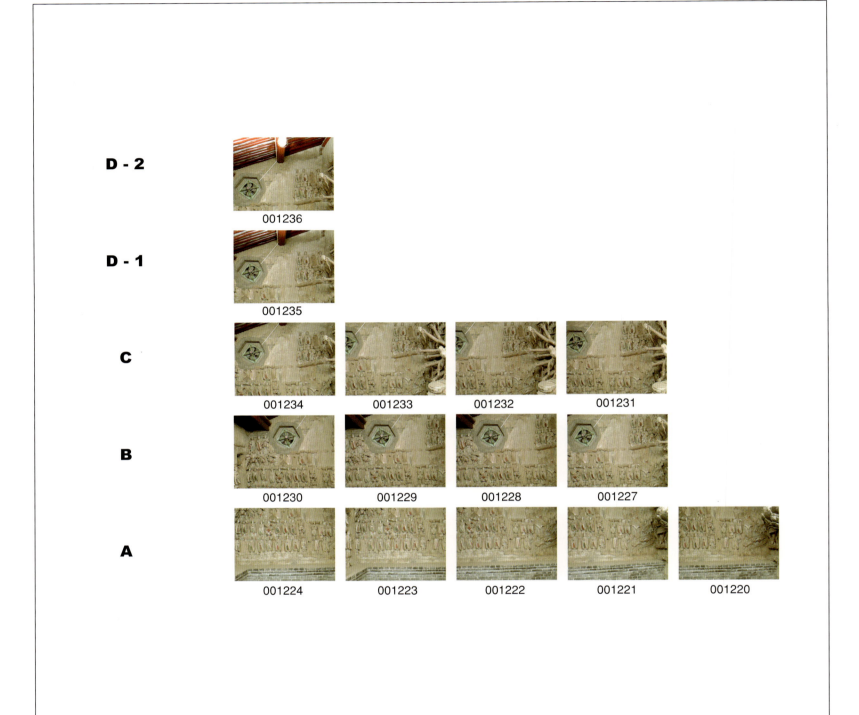

35   北山墙西南壁

North Wall, Rear Chamber

高：2.8～4.3 米，宽：3.2 米，15 张单幅照片

H：2.8～4.3m，W：3.2m，15 photographs

这部分彩绘壁塑和西后檐墙、南山墙西北壁为一组壁塑，均为"佛升忉利天为母摩耶夫人说法"。塑像有四层，人物塑像均为聆听佛法的信众。

　　The sculptures along this surface, together with those along the West Wall and South Wall of the Rear Chamber, form a group portraying the Jātaka Tale, "Buddha ascends Trāyastriṃśas to preach to Queen Māyā". The sculptures of human figures on this surface are arranged in four horizontal tiers and portray followers listening to Buddha's preaching.

36 信众
Followers

D　CF001724　CF001725　CF001726　CF001727　CF001728　CF001729　CF001730　CF001731　CF0017

C　CF001639　CF001640　CF001641　CF001661　CF001662　CF001642　CF001643　CF001644　CF001645　CF001646　CF001663　CF001647　CF001648　CF0016

B　CF001604　CF001605　CF001606　CF001607　CF001609　CF001610　CF001611　CF001612　CF001613　CF001614　CF001615　CF001616　CF001617　CF001618　CF00161

A　CF001564　CF001565　CF001566　CF001567　CF001569　CF001570　CF001571　CF001572　CF001573　CF001574　CF001575　CF001576　CF001577　CF001578　CF00157

37　西后檐墙东壁

West Wall, Rear Chamber

高：2.8米，宽：17.6米，131张单幅照片

H：2.8m，W：3.2m，131 photographs

　　这部分彩绘壁塑和北山墙西南壁、南山墙西北壁为一组壁塑，均为"佛升忉利天为母摩耶夫人说法"。这面的塑像有四层，正中塑有一佛龛，龛内塑释迦牟尼坐莲台上，左右立有迦叶和阿难，佛母摩耶夫人面佛跪于神兽扛着的莲台上，周围均为聆听佛法的信众。

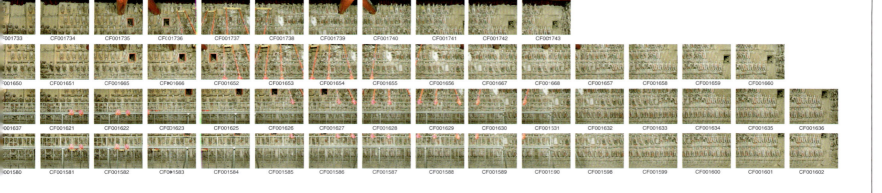

The sculptures along this surface, together with those along the North Wall and South Wall, of the Rear Chamber, form a group portraying the Jātaka Tale "Buddha ascends Trāyastrimśas to preach to Queen Māyā". The sculptures on this surface are arranged in four horizontal tiers. The center niche contains a statue of Śākyamuni seated on a lotus throne which is supported by mythical beasts. Kāśyapa is to his right and Ānanda to his left. Queen Māyā kneels before him, and they are surrounded by followers listening to Buddha's preaching.

39 释迦牟尼、阿难、迦叶、摩耶夫人
Śākyamuni, Ānanda, Kāśyapa, Queen Māyā

38 佛升忉利天为母摩耶夫人说法、信众

Buddha ascends Trāyastrimśas to preach to Queen Māyā and followers

40 信众
Followers

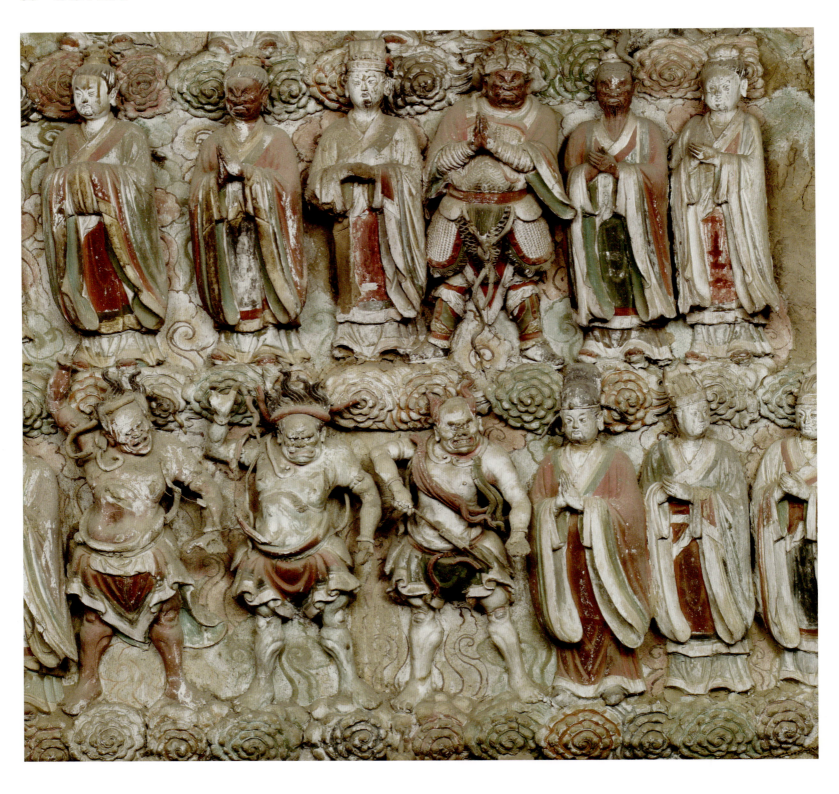

41 信众
Followers

42 信众
Followers

43 信众
Followers

B - 3

CF001812

B - 2

CF001811

B - 1

CF001806   CF001807   CF001808   CF001809

A

CF001800   CF001803   CF001801   CF001802

44   南山墙西北壁

South Wall, Rear Chamber

高：2.8～4.3 米，宽：3.2 米，10 张单幅照片

H：2.8m，W：3.2m，10 photographs

这部分彩绘壁塑和西后檐墙、北山墙西南壁为一组壁塑，均为"佛升忉利天为母摩耶夫人说法"。这面的塑像有四层，人物塑像均为聆听佛法的信众。

The sculptures along this surface, together with those along the North Wall and West Wall of the Rear Chamber, form a group portraying the Jātaka Tale, "Buddha ascends Trāyastrimśas to preach to Queen Māyā". The sculptures of human figures on this surface are arranged in four horizontal tiers and portray followers listening to Buddha's preaching.

45 信众
Followers

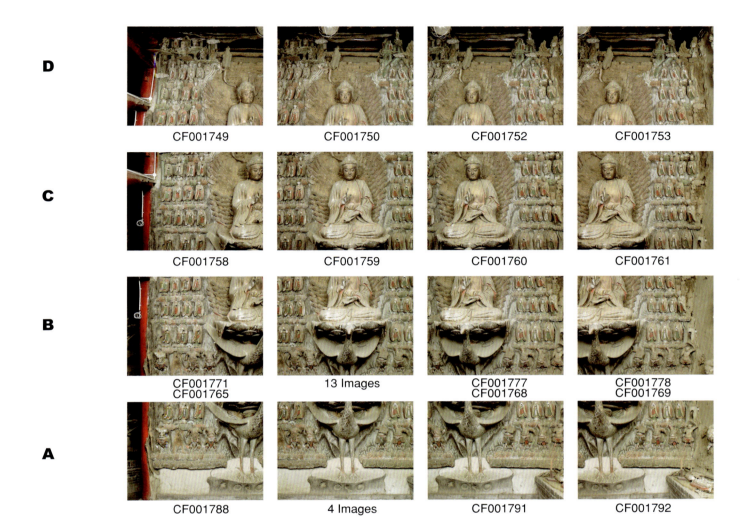

D | CF001749 | CF001750 | CF001752 | CF001753

C | CF001758 | CF001759 | CF001760 | CF001761

B | CF001771 / CF001765 | 13 Images | CF001777 / CF001768 | CF001778 / CF001769

A | CF001788 | 4 Images | CF001791 | CF001792

46 南梢间横墙西壁

South East Wall, Rear Chamber

高：4.3 米，宽：3.2 米，16 张单幅照片

H：4.3m，W：3.2m，16 photographs

这部分彩绘泥塑主佛文殊菩萨居中，也称阿弥陀佛。菩萨坐于孔雀背负的莲台之上，背有孔雀尾佛光。其周围分六层，塑有护法金刚力士和供养人立于云朵上。

The main statue in this section is one of Mañjuśrī, or possibly Amitābha, seated on a lotus throne supported by a peacock. The halo behind the statue is composed of peacock tail feathers. The surrounding area is arranged in six horizontal tiers featuring sculptures of guardian figures and attendants standing atop clouds.

47 文殊菩萨（也有称阿弥陀佛）
Mañjuśrī (or possibly Amitābha)

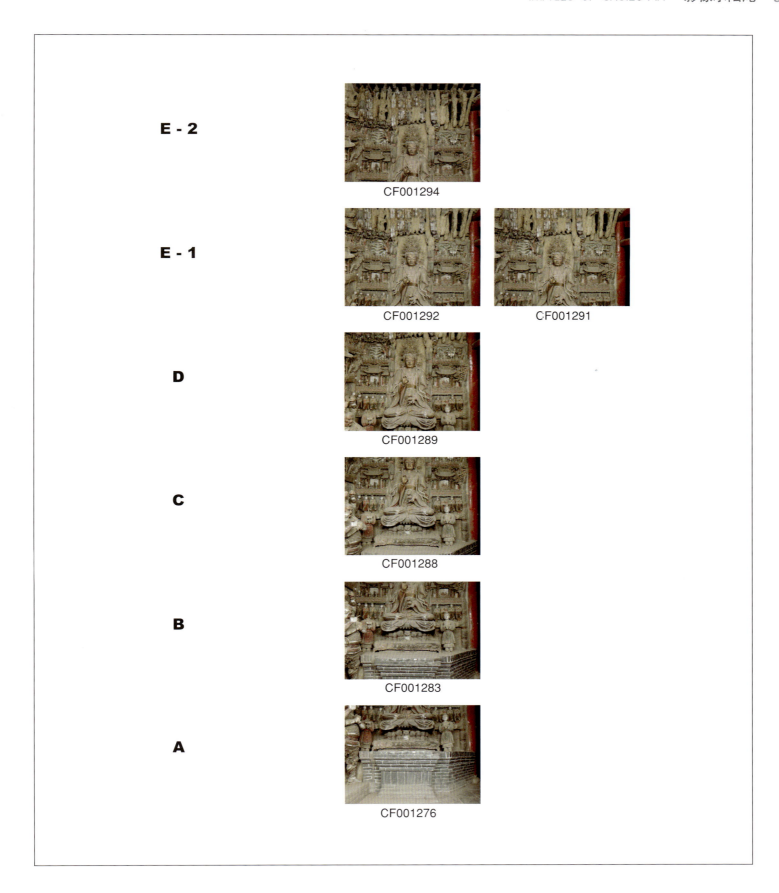

E - 2

CF001294

E - 1

CF001292 · CF001291

D

CF001289

C

CF001288

B

CF001283

A

CF001276

48 南梢间横墙东壁

South Wall West, Front Chamber

高：4.3 米，宽：3.2 米，7 张单幅照片

H：4.3m，W：3.2m，7 photographs

这部分彩绘泥塑主佛药王菩萨居中，头戴五佛宝冠，左手持葫芦，下坐石台。座下有一龛，龛内有一狮子。背后上端壁画已残损，身旁左右各塑立一侍者。周围有亭台楼阁、山水人物及药王经变故事。

The main statue in this section is Bhaisajya-rāja Bodhisattva, wearing a Buddha-crown containing the Five Dhyāni-Buddhas, seated on a stone dais. His left hand holds a bottle gourd. Below the stone dais is a niche with a lion. The upper section of the wall painting behind the statue is badly damaged. The statue is flanked by two attendants and is surrounded by balconies, pavilions, landscapes, human figures and tales from the Bhaisajya-rāja Bodhisattva Sūtra.

49 药王菩萨
Bhaisajya-rāja Bodhisattva

50 药王菩萨（局部）
Bhaisajya-rāja Bodhisattva (Partial)

N Tilt   CF000879   CF000872   CF000873   CF000874

N   CF000864   CF000865   CF000866

M   CF000860   CF000861   CF000853   CF000854

L   CF000819   CF000820   CF000821   CF000834   CF000835   CF000836

K   CF000802   CF000803   CF000804   CF000805   CF000806   CF000808   CF000809

J   CF000758   CF000756   CF000784   CF000785   CF000786   CF000787   CF000788   CF000789   CF000790

I   CF000748   CF000749   CF000750   CF000752   CF000764   CF000765   CF000766   CF000767   CF000768   CF000769   CF000770

H   CF000724   CF000725   CF000726   CF000727   CF000728   CF000729   CF000730   CF000731   CF000732   CF000733

G   CF000699   CF000700   CF000701   CF000702   CF000703   CF000704   CF000705   CF000706   CF000707   CF000708

F   CF000676   CF000677   CF000678   CF000679   CF000680   CF000681   CF000682   CF000683   CF000684   CF000685

E   CF000650   CF000651   CF000652   CF000653   CF000654   CF000655   CF000656   CF000657   CF000658   CF000659

D   CF000636   CF000637   CF000638   CF000639   CF000640   CF000641

C   CF000614   CF000615   CF000616   CF000617   CF000618   CF000619

B   CF000598   CF000599   CF000600   CF000601   CF000612   CF000613

A   CF000574   CF000575   CF000576   CF000577   CF000578   CF000580

51 南山墙东北壁

South Wall, Front Chamber

高：7.4 米，宽：11.0 米，231 张单幅照片

H：7.4m，W：11.0m，231 photographs

这部分彩绘泥塑由下至上，第一层二十四诸神，也有称为天龙八部，塑有十二尊，与北山墙合为二十四尊。这组塑像有的两头两臂，有的三头六臂，有的四头八臂，有的手持利刃，高举法器，有的足踩怪物。第二层塑五百罗汉过海与北山墙合为一整体。第二层以上是以正中二重庑殿为中心，主要塑有佛陀涅槃的佛传故事，与北山墙佛陀降生对应。在二重庑殿内，释迦牟尼倒卧在床上，迦叶、阿难、舍利佛、目犍连、阿那律、富楼那、须普提、迦旃延、邬波离、罗睺罗等十大弟子和两个护法金刚力士守护在佛的周围。该壁的右上方中层有诵经拜塔等佛教诵经说法的场景。

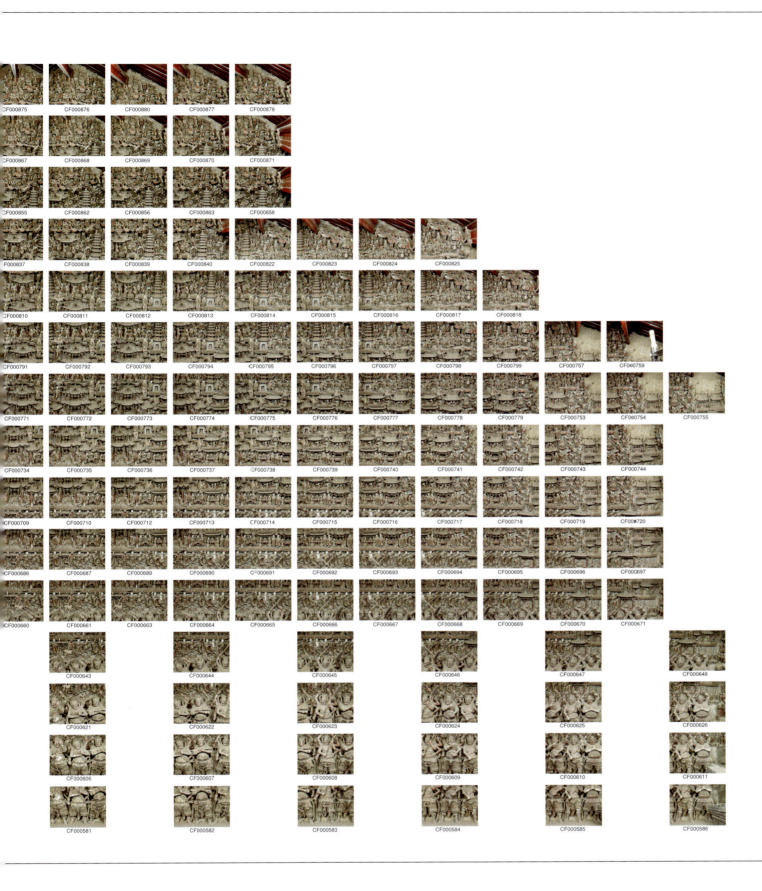

From bottom to top in this section: the first tier contains the twenty-four Divine Guardians, also known as the Eight Classes of Beings. There are twelve statues on this side and twelve more along the North Wall. Some statues are two-armed and two-headed, some six-armed and three-headed, and some eight-armed and four-headed. Some are holding sharp weapons, some are raising ritual objects aloft, and others are trampling on monsters. The statues of the Five Hundred Arhats on the second tier form a complete whole together with those along the North Wall. In the center above the second tier is 2-story building with a hip roof illustrating the Parinirvāna story. This is paired with the "Descent into the world" story on the North Wall. "Parinirvāna": inside the building, Śākyamuni lies on a bed. He is surrounded by his ten chief disciples--Kāśyapa, Ānanda, Śāriputra, Maudgalyāyana, Aniruddha, Pūrnamaitrāyanīputra, Subhuti, Kātyāyana, Upananda, and Rāhula--and two guardians. In the middle tier of the upper right section, there is a preaching scene, with followers chanting sūtras and circumambulating a pagoda.

53 十二尊神将、罗汉过海 12 Divine Guardians, Arhats Crossing the Sea

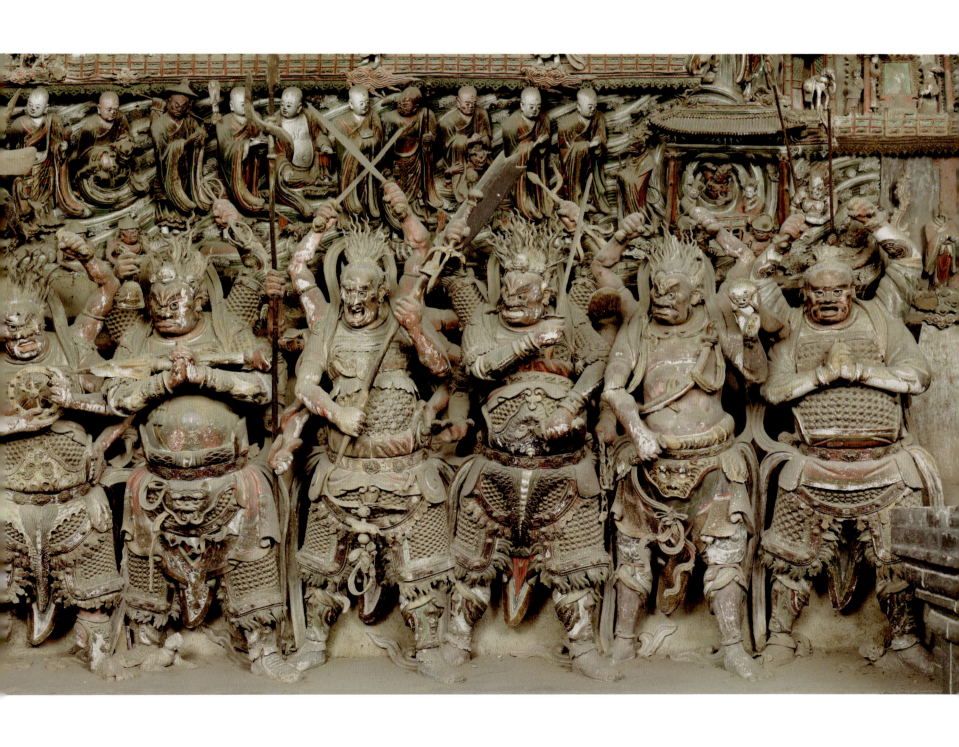

54 十二尊神将（局部）
12 Divine Guardians (Partial)

55 十二尊神将（局部）
12 Divine Guardians (Partial)

56 十二尊神将（局部）
12 Divine Guardians (Partial)

57　十二尊神将（局部）
12 Divine Guardians (Partial)

58 十二尊神将（局部）
12 Divine Guardians (Partial)

59　十二尊神将（局部）
12 Divine Guardians (Partial)

60 南山墙东北壁（局部）
South Wall, Front Chamber (Partial)

61 南山墙东北壁（局部）
South Wall, Front Chamber (Partial)

62　南山墙东北壁（局部）
South Wall, Front Chamber (Partial)

64 南山墙东北壁（局部）
South Wall, Front Chamber (Partial)

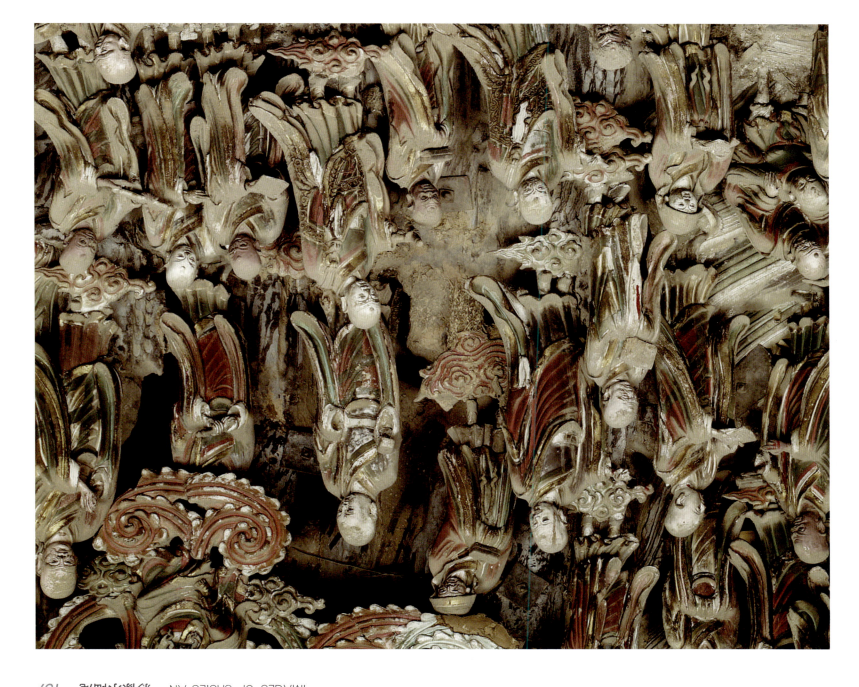

66　涅槃
Parinirvāna

67 庵婆罗丽
Mrapālī

69   拈花微笑
Buddha holds up a flower as Kāśyapa smiles

70   诵经拜塔
Chanting sutras and circumambulating a pagoda

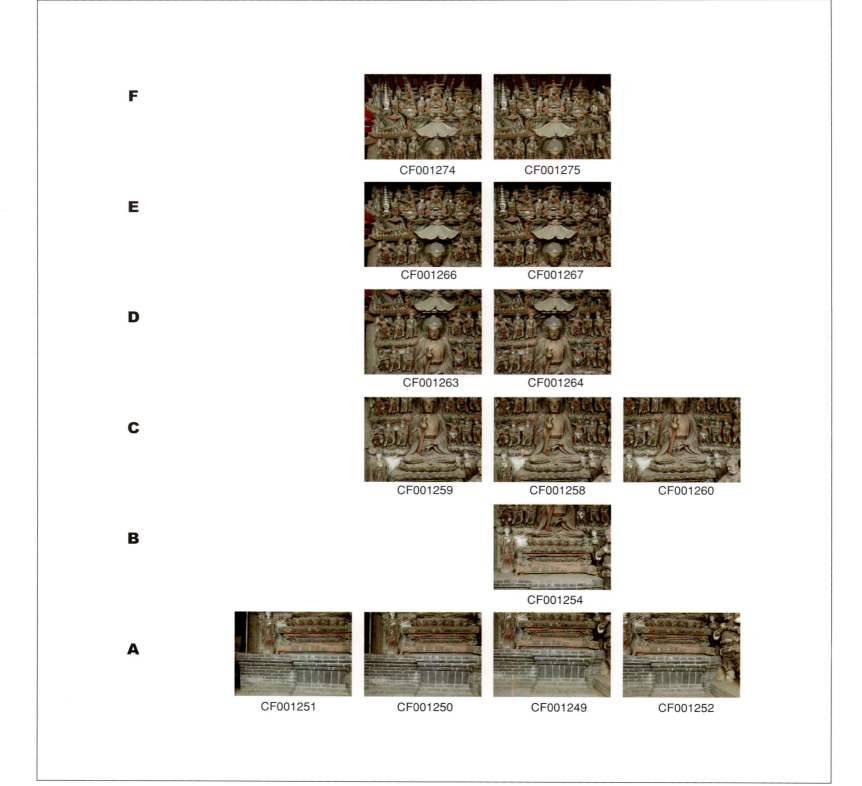

F CF001274 CF001275

E CF001266 CF001267

D CF001263 CF001264

C CF001259 CF001258 CF001260

B CF001254

A CF001251 CF001250 CF001249 CF001252

71 东前檐墙南梢间西壁

South Wall East, Front Chamber

高：4.3米，宽：3.2米，14张单幅照片

H：4.3m，W：3.2m，14 photographs

这部分彩绘泥塑主佛释迦牟尼居中，下坐莲台，上擎幡盖，后有背光，左右各立一侍者。周围分三层，由下至上，第一、二层塑护法金刚力士，站立云头，有的手持法器，有的抱拳合掌；第三层幡盖周围有供养人等。主佛上方中为释迦牟尼，坐云上莲台，左右塑立阿难和迦叶，北面有大势至菩萨，右塑一侍者立于云上；南面塑有观世音菩萨，其左塑善财童子立于云上。

　　This section features a central statue of Śākyamuni seated on a lotus throne, with a patākā shade overhead and a halo behind him. He is flanked on each side by an attendant. The adjacent area is arranged in three horizontal tiers. From bottom to top: on the first and second tiers, guardians protecting the Buddha stand upon clouds. Some wield ritual objects; others hold their palms together. On the third tier, attendants surround the patākā shade. Above the main statue, there is a smaller Śākyamuni seated on a lotus throne, with Ānanda on his left and Kāśyapa on his right. The statue on the north side is Mahāsthāmaprāpta, with an attendant to his right standing on a cloud. The statue on the south side is Avalokiteśvara, with Sudhana to his left standing on a cloud.

72 释迦牟尼
Śākyamuni

73 释迦牟尼、阿难、迦叶
Śākyamuni, Ānanda, Kāśyapa

75　大势至菩萨
Mahāsthānmaprāpta

76 观音菩萨、善财童子
Avalokiteśvara, Sudhana

Severe Tilt		CF001152	CF001153	CF001154	CF001155	CF001156	CF001157	CF001158	CF001159	CF001160	CF00116
H - Near 2		CF001192	CF001193	CF001194	CF001195	CF001196	CF001216	CF001
H - Near 1		CF001182	CF001187	CF001183	CF001188	CF001184	CF001189	CF001185	CF001190	CF0011
H - Far		CF001205	CF001206	CF001207	CF001208	CF0012
G		CF001174	CF001175	CF001176	CF001177	CF001178	CF001199	CF001
F		CF001125	CF001126	CF001127	CF001128	CF001129	CF001130	CF001131	CF001132	CF001133	CF0011
E		CF001098	CF001099	CF001095	CF001100	CF001101	CF001102	CF001103	CF001104	CF001105	CF001106	CF001
D - Near	CF001034	CF001058	CF001035	CF001036	CF001037	CF001038	CF001059	CF001039	CF001040	CF001041	CF001063	CF001
D - Far		CF001065	CF001066	CF001067	CF001068	CF001069	CF001070	CF001071	CF001072	CF001073	CF0010
C - Near		CF000986	CF000988	CF000989	CF000990	CF000991	CF000992	CF000993	CF000994	CF000995	CF0009
C - Far		CF001009	CF001010	CF001011	CF001012	CF001013	CF001014	CF001015	CF001016	CF001017	CF0010
B - Near	CF000960	CF000959	CF000938	CF000939	CF000961	CF000940	CF000941	CF000942	CF000943	CF000944	CF000945	CF3009
B - Far		CF000964	CF000965	CF000966	CF000967	CF000968	CF000969	CF000970	CF000971	CF000972	CF0009
B - Brick		CF000917	CF000918	CF000919	CF000920	CF000921	CF000922	CF000
A		CF000892	CF000893	CF000894	CF000895	CF000896	CF000897	CF000

77 背光墙东壁

West Wall, Front Chamber

高：5.7 米，宽：11.2 米，269 张单幅照片

H：5.7m，W：11.2m，269 photographs

这部分彩绘泥塑是"横三世佛"。中为释迦牟尼佛，下坐三级莲台，在第二级正中有"万国礼佛"壁画，北面有"佛像士山西匠人乔仲超"的题刻，由四力士扛座。佛上方有华盖，左右塑立迦叶和阿难，背后有大型背光。背光内容丰富，以主佛为中心，第一、二层为佛光外轮，由火焰纹与飞龙组成；第三、四、五层为花带纹，上有诸佛菩萨、乐人、护法等悬塑；第五层带纹以内为中心，主要塑有宝相花，并有鳌鱼、午象、立羊等瑞兽于其间。主佛上端塑"大鹏金翅雕"、"鬼子母"等佛教经变故事。北为阿弥陀佛，下坐三级莲台，左右立两侍者，背光结构与释迦牟尼后背光大体相同，也有诸佛菩萨、乐人、护法等。另外，还塑有大势至菩萨和观世音菩萨，与主佛合为"西方三圣"。南为药师琉璃佛，下坐三级莲台，左右塑立两侍者，背光结构与释迦牟尼后背光大体相同，也有诸佛菩萨、乐人、护法等。此外，还有日光遍照菩萨和月光遍照菩萨，与主佛合为"东方三圣"。

The section depicts the "Horizontal Buddhas in Three Manifestations". Śākyamuni, center, sits on a three-tiered lotus throne. At the center of the second tier, there is a wall painting showing followers from many countries paying respects to Buddha. An inscription on the north side states that Shanxi craftsman Qiao Zhongchao created the Buddha statues. The lotus throne is held up by four muscular guardians. A baldachin shelters Śākyamuni, who has Kāśyapa to his left, Ānanda to his right, and a large halo behind him. The halo is richly detailed. With Śākyamuni at its center, its first and second layers form the outermost rings of the halo, and these are composed of a flame pattern intertwined with flying dragons. The third, fourth and fifth layers have floral motifs with suspended sculptures of Buddhas, bodhisattvas, musicians, and guardians. Within the fifth layer, the main sculptural motifs include the baoxiang floral pattern, turtles, fishes, elephants, goats and other auspicious animals. Above Śākyamuni are sculptures depicting the "Golden-winged Garuda", "Hāritī" and other sūtra tales. On the north side of Śākyamuni is Amitābha, seated on a three-tiered lotus throne and flanked on each side by an attendant. The design of his halo is generally similar to that of Śākyamuni's, and also features suspended sculptures of Buddhas, bodhisattvas, musicians and guardians. There are also sculptures of, Mahāsthāmaprāpta and Avalokiteśvara, who, together with one of Amitābha, make up the "Three Sages of the West". On the south side of Śākyamuni is Bhaisajyaguru Buddha, seated on a three-tiered lotus throne and flanked on each side by an attendant. The design of his halo is generally similar to that of Śākyamuni' s, and also features suspended sculptures of Buddhas, bodhisattvas, musicians and guardians. There are also sculptures of the Sunlight Bodhisattva and Moonlight Bodhisattva, who, together with one of Bhaisajyaguru Buddha, make up the "Three Sages of the East".

78　释迦牟尼佛、阿弥陀佛、药师琉璃佛　Śākyamuni, Amitābha, Bhaisajyaguru Buddha

82　韦驮、鬼子母、大鹏金翅雕
Weiduo, Hārītī, Golden-winged Garuda

83 东方三圣：日光遍照菩萨、月光遍照菩萨、东方药师佛
The Three Sages of the East：the Sunlight Bodhisattva, Moonlight Bodhisattva and Bhaisajyaguru Buddha

84 大鹏金翅雕、四世佛
Golden-winged Garuda, Buddha's earthly life

85　瑞兽
Auspicious animal

86　大鹏金翅雕
Golden-winged Garuda

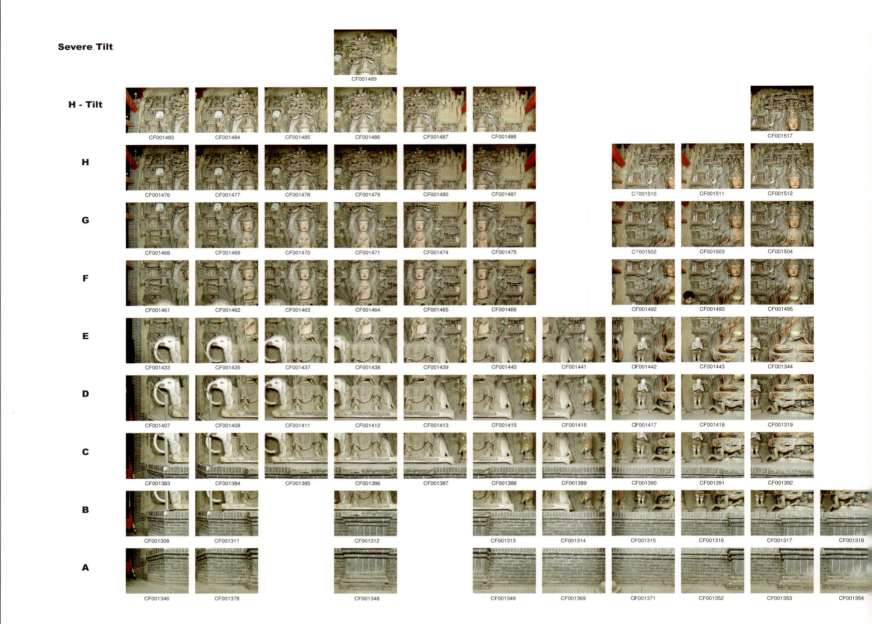

87 背光墙西壁

East Wall, Rear Chamber

高：5.7 米，宽：11.2 米，184 张单幅照片

H：5.7m， W：11.2m， 184 photographs

这部分彩绘泥塑是"三大菩萨"。中为观世音菩萨，坐于龙台之上。龙台上为复莲台。菩萨上方有华盖，背有背光，左右塑立善财童子和吒叱，周围塑有净瓶、白鸽等。整个墙面还塑有殿宇楼阁、珍宝和人物，是"善财童子五十三参"的佛教经变故事。观世音菩萨北为普贤菩萨，下坐白象；南为文殊菩萨，下坐狮子。其上方均有幡盖和背光。

This section depicts the "Three Great Bodhisattvas". Avalokiteśvara, center, sits on a dragon throne, which in turn supports a lotus throne. There is a baldachin above him and a halo behind; Sudhana and Zhachi flank the statue. The adjacent sculptures includes a purity bottle and white dove. Around each of the "Three Great Bodhisattvas" there are pavilions, balconies, precious treasures and human figures--all depicting tales from the Avatamsakasūtra (Flower Garland Sūtra). To the north of Avalokiteśvara is Samantabhadra riding a white elephant, and to the south is Mañjuśrī riding a lion. There are patākā shades above them and halos behind them.

88　观世音菩萨、普贤菩萨、文殊菩萨　Avalokiteśvara, Samantabhadra, Mañjuśrī

89 观世音菩萨（二维高清晰单幅图片：5436 × 4080 像素 / 张）
Avalokiteśvara (64 Mb/Raw 文件 Single high-resolution 2D image: 5436 × 4080 pixels, 64 Mb Raw file)

90 观世音菩萨（二维高清晰图片局部原大：细节清晰可见）
Avalokiteśvara (Enlarged section of high-resolution 2D image: details can be clearly seen)

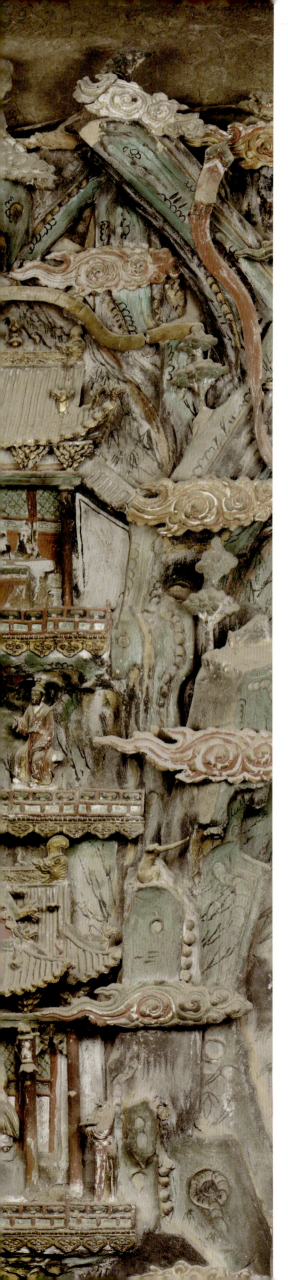

91 善财童子五十三参
53 Visits of Sudhana

92 龙台
Dragon Throne

93 龙台（局部）
Dragon Throne (Partail)

94 供养人
Attendant

贰　虚拟现实摄影

　　虚拟漫游 (Virtual Reality)是通过由计算机硬件、软件以及各种传感器构成三维信息的人工环境——虚拟环境。这种虚拟环境是使用者在视、听、触、嗅等感知行为处于虚拟三维的逼真体验中。通常在文物领域，主要使用的是三维全景虚拟现实（也称实景虚拟），这种技术是在数字摄影技术的基础上，使用特殊的拍摄器材和专门的计算机软件得以实现。

　　根据水陆庵水陆殿建筑和泥塑群的布局,在水陆庵的虚拟漫游图像的拍摄时，选择了七个图像采集点，共拍摄数码照片268幅，每幅照片4992 × 3320（1600万）像素，原始数据达18GB。通过营造良好的自然光照效果和各个机位、角度的数字摄影，制作的360度泥塑群的虚拟漫游，使参观、浏览及研究有身临其境的感觉，做到了参观路线与泥塑内容的统一。

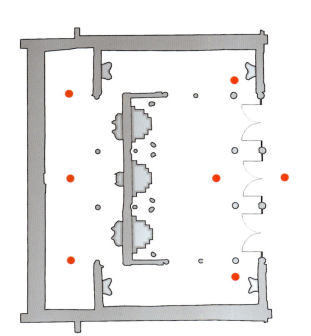

虚拟漫游七个图像采集点分布图

Locations of the 7 image capture points for VR production

II. Virtual Reality images（VR's）

　　Virtual Reality is an artificial environment -- a virtual environment--created with three dimensional information from computer hardware, software and various sensory transmission devices. Such virtual environments cause the user to have a realistic experience through use of the senses, such as vision, hearing, touch or smell. In work related to cultural objects, the primary type of virtual reality used is three-dimensional virtual panoramic reality (virtual scenes.) This technique is based on a foundation of digital photography, and is implemented through the use of special photographic apparatus and computer software.

　　Taking into account the layout of the Shuilu Pavilion building and the clay sculptures within it, seven nodes were selected as image capture points for the shooting of the Shuilu'an VR's. A total of 268 photographs were taken, each one 4992 × 3320 (16 million) pixels, yielding 18 Gb of raw data. Through the creation of good naturalistic lighting effects and digital photography from a variety of camera locations and angles, the 360° VR's of the clay sculptures impart a "you-are-there" sensation of visiting, browsing and studying, and achieve a unity between the route of travel and the content of the sculptures.

Up

60

0

-60

Down

XF4X2315

XF4X2469　XF4X2476　XF4X2482　XF4X2481　XF4X2480　XF4X2471

XF4X2447　XF4X2457　XF4X2465　XF4X2464　XF4X2461　XF4X2451

XF4X2490　XF4X2495　XF4X2494　XF4X2493　XF4X2492　XF4X2491

XF4X2497

95 水陆殿殿外虚拟漫游：20 张单幅照片
VR of exterior of the Shuilu Pavilion：20 photographs

水陆殿殿外虚拟漫游：360 度二维图像
VR of exterior of the Shuilu Pavilion：360-degree 2D image

96　水陆殿殿外虚拟漫游：360 度二维图像
VR of exterior of the Shuilu Pavilion：360-degree 2D image

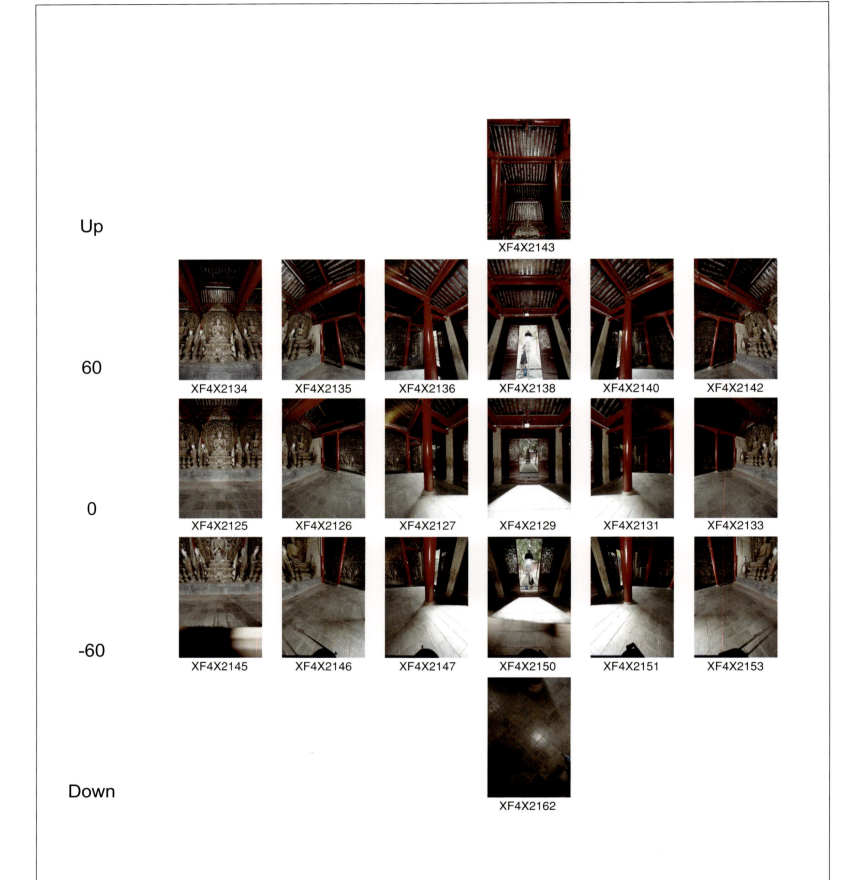

Up

60

0

-60

Down

XF4X2143

XF4X2134　XF4X2135　XF4X2136　XF4X2138　XF4X2140　XF4X2142

XF4X2125　XF4X2126　XF4X2127　XF4X2129　XF4X2131　XF4X2133

XF4X2145　XF4X2146　XF4X2147　XF4X2150　XF4X2151　XF4X2153

XF4X2162

97 水陆殿前殿虚拟漫游：20 张单幅照片

VR of the front chamber of the Shuilu Pavilion：20 photographs

水陆殿前殿虚拟漫游：360 度二维图像

98　水陆殿前殿虚拟漫游：360 度二维图像
VR of the front chamber of the Shuilu Pavilion：360-degree 2D image

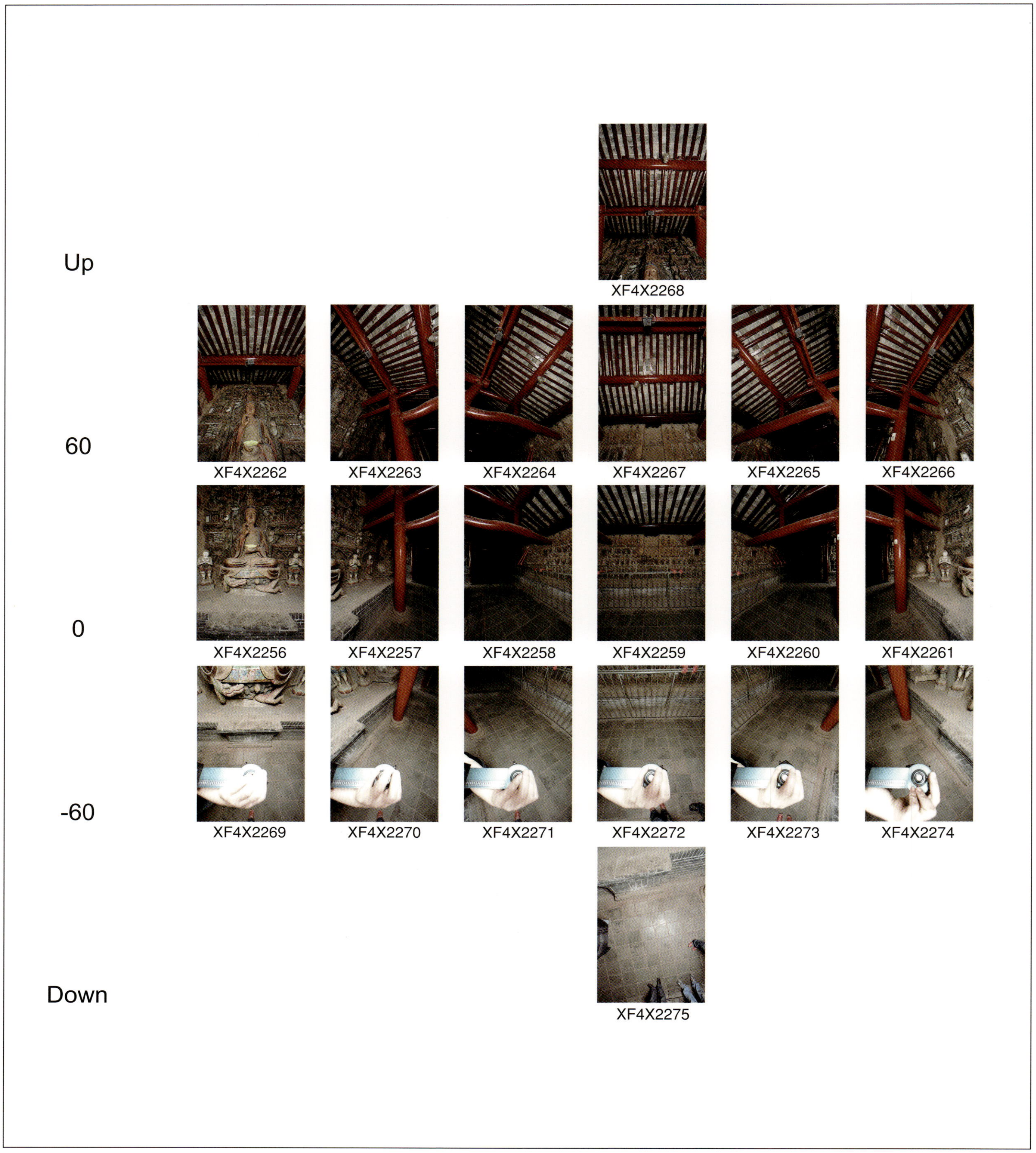

Up

60

0

-60

Down

XF4X2268

XF4X2262 XF4X2263 XF4X2264 XF4X2267 XF4X2265 XF4X2266

XF4X2256 XF4X2257 XF4X2258 XF4X2259 XF4X2260 XF4X2261

XF4X2269 XF4X2270 XF4X2271 XF4X2272 XF4X2273 XF4X2274

XF4X2275

99 水陆殿后殿虚拟漫游：20 张单幅照片
VR of the rear chamber of the Shuilu Pavilion：20 photographs

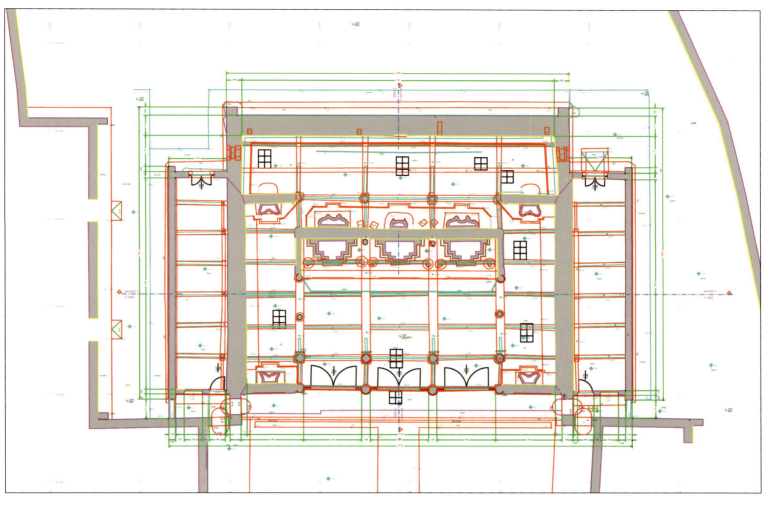

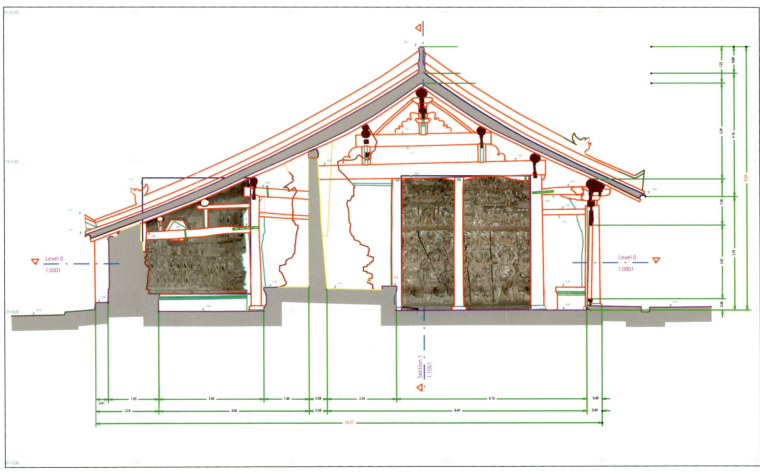

101　由三维模型得到的水陆殿平面图
Floor plan of the Shuilu Pavilion derived from 3D model

102　由三维模型得到的水陆殿横剖面图
Horizontal section of the Shuilu Pavilion derived from 3D model

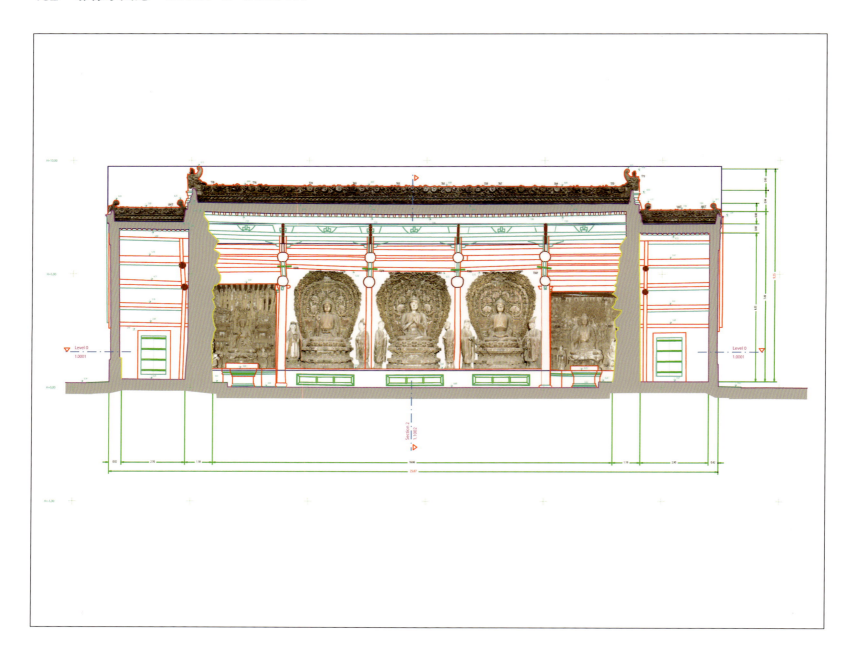

103 由三维模型得到的水陆殿纵剖面图
Vertical section of the Shuilu Pavilion derived from 3D model

104 水陆殿及北山墙部分泥塑三维模型：殿前视角线图
3D model of the Shuilu Pavilion and a portion of the sculptures along the North Wall perspective：drawing from front of Pavilion

105 水陆殿三维模型：殿前视角渲染图
3D model of the Shuilu Pavilion：rendering from front of Pavilion

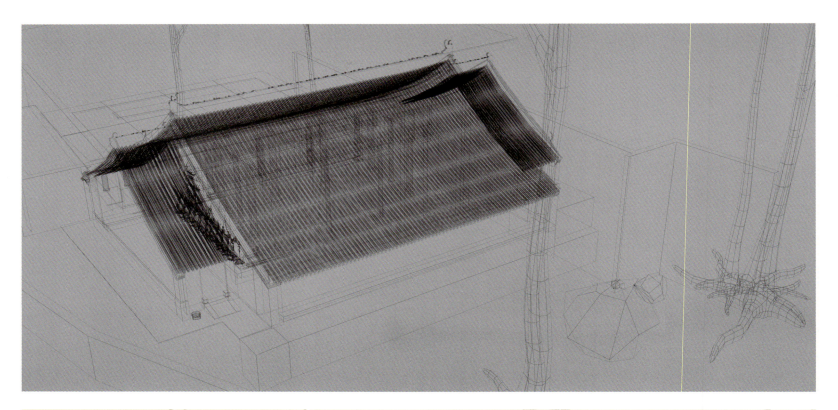

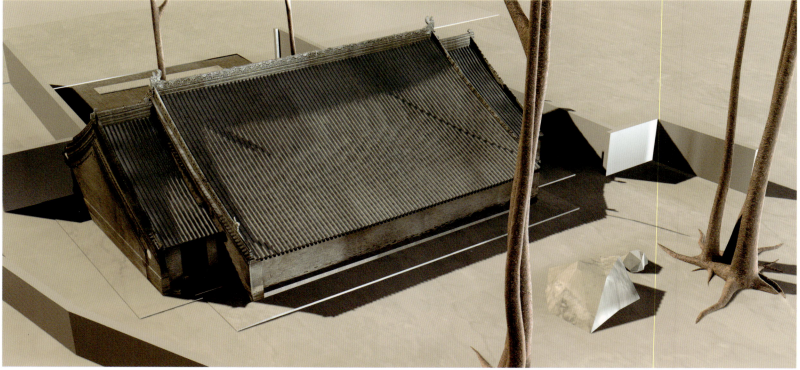

106　水陆殿及北山墙部分泥塑三维模型：殿后视角线图
　　3D model of the Shuilu Pavilion and a portion of the sculptures along the
　　North Wall：perspective drawing from rear of Pavilion

107　水陆殿三维模型：殿后视角渲染图
　　3D model of the Shuilu Pavilion：rendering from rear of Pavilion

108　水陆殿及北山墙部分泥塑三维模型：殿内视角线图
3D model of the Shuilu Pavilion and a portion of the sculptures along the
north wall：perspective drawing from interior of Pavilion

109 水陆殿及北山墙部分泥塑三维模型：殿内视角渲染图
3D model of the Shuilu Pavilion and a portion of the sculptures along the north wall：rendering of interior of Pavilion

肆　三维扫描

泥塑三维模型
3D model of clay sculpture

三维扫描就是测量有形物体表面的三维坐标数据，而每一个数据（点）都带有相应的 x、y、z 坐标数值，这些数据（点）集合起来形成的点云（Point Cloud），就能构成物体表面的特征。它是通过三维激光扫描仪或者三坐标测量仪对物体表面进行三维的扫描或测量，获得物体的三维点云数据，再利用逆向工程软件对获得的三维扫描数据进行整理、编辑、获取所需的三维特征曲线，最终通过三维曲面表达出物体的外形。随着三维扫描技术的发展，其扫描精度已能达到毫米乃至微米级。

高精度的三维扫描技术应用到像水陆庵大面积、大数量、错落不齐的立体彩色泥塑群上，在世界上目前可能属于首次。无论是现场的扫描数据收集，还是后期制作处理，都是一个大数据量、拼合精细、极具挑战性的数字化图像的科研攻关课题，是一次有意义的尝试。

Ⅳ. 3D Scanning

A 3D scan measures the three-dimensional coordinates of the surfaces of a material object, and each piece (point) of data includes corresponding values for the x, y and z coordinates. Together this data (points) from a point cloud captures the features of the object's surfaces. The 3D point cloud data is obtained through 3D scanning or measuring, either with a 3D laser scanner or with equipment which measures the three coordinates. The point cloud is then sorted and edited with reverse engineering software to yield the necessary 3D contours, and finally the 3D contours are used to show the external shape of the object. With the development of 3D scanning technology, scans of a millimeter or finer are now possible.

The use of high-precision 3D laser scanning on sculptures as large in area, as numerous, and as irregularly arranged as those at Shuilu'an may have been the first attempt of this sort in the world. Both the on-site data collection and the postproduction work involved large volumes of data and precise matching. As an extremely challenging effort in digital imaging, this endeavor had special significance.

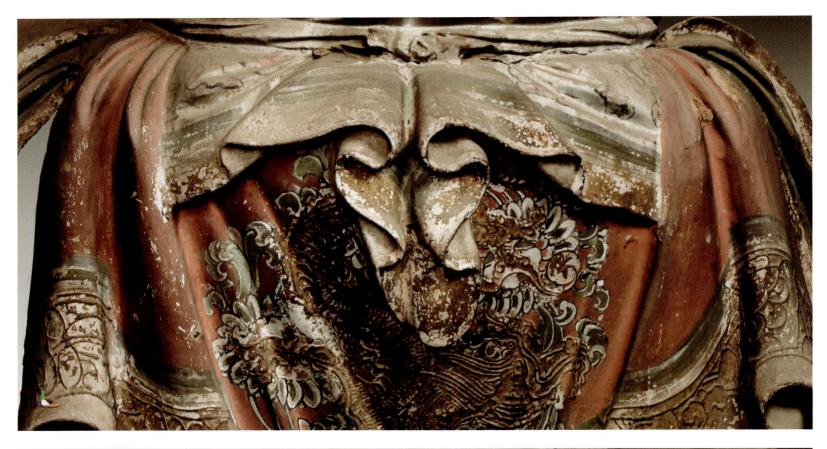

110　泥塑三维模型腰部
　　　　3D model of midsection of clay sculpture

111　泥塑三维模型脸部
　　　　3D model of face of clay sculpture

112 三维模型点云图
Point cloud of 3D model

113 三维模型点线面图
3D mesh of face of clay sculpture

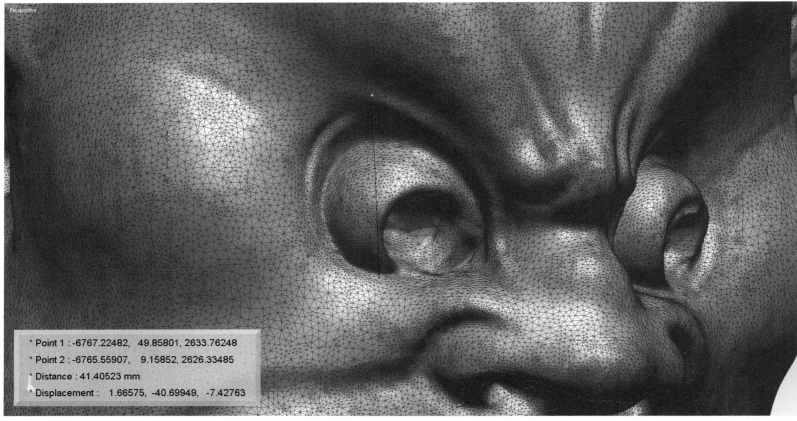

* Point 1 : -6767.22482,   49.85801, 2633.76248
* Point 2 : -6765.55907,   9.15852, 2626.33485
* Distance : 41.40523 mm
* Displacement :   1.66575, -40.69949, -7.42763

114 三维模型点云成面图
    3D texture of face of clay sculpture

115 三维模型点线面眼部图
    3D mesh of eyes of clay sculpture

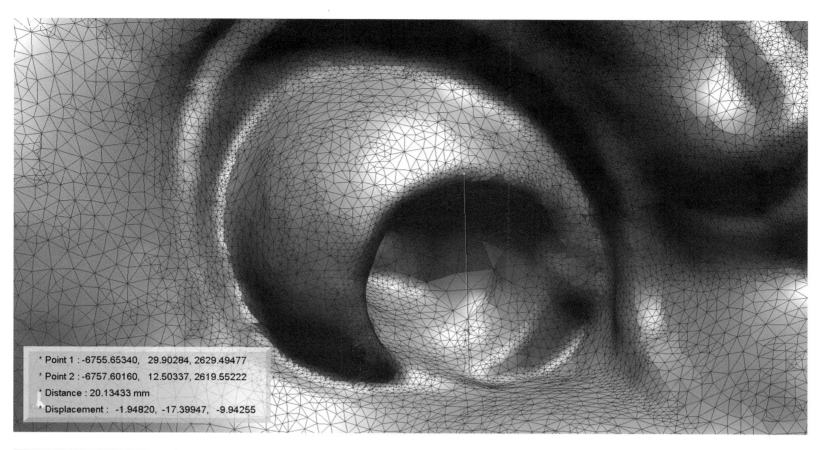

* Point 1 : -6755.65340,　29.90284, 2629.49477
* Point 2 : -6757.60160,　12.50337, 2619.55222
* Distance : 20.13433 mm
* Displacement :　-1.94820, -17.39947,　-9.94255

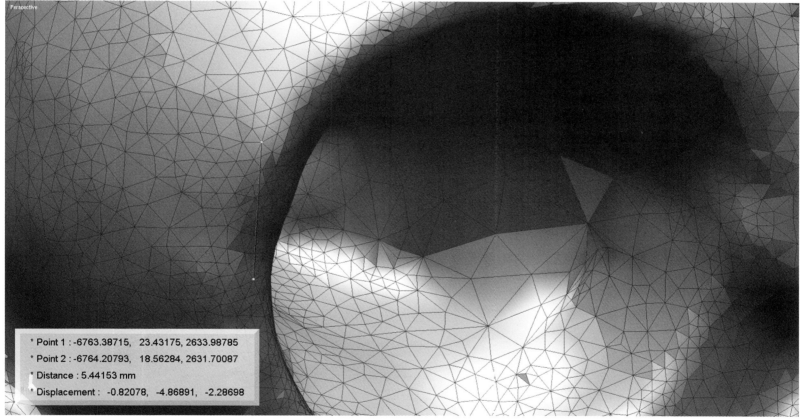

Perspective

* Point 1 : -6763.38715,　23.43175, 2633.98785
* Point 2 : -6764.20793,　18.56284, 2631.70087
* Distance : 5.44153 mm
* Displacement :　-0.82078,　-4.86891,　-2.28698

116　三维模型点线面眼部放大图
　　　Enlargement of 3D mesh of eye of clay sculpture

117　三维模型点线面瞳孔放大图
　　　Enlargement of 3D mesh of eye socket of clay sculpture

伍　基于互联网的数据
　　　整合及共享

　　当今，互联网已经成为全球信息共享的主要途经。文物的特殊性决定了文物"数字化"必然会产生海量的信息。如何通过互联网，使人们能够便利地访问各类文物信息，成为文物数字化利用和文物信息传播的瓶颈。对此，本项目通过对形成的海量水陆庵数字化信息：建筑及泥塑历史背景、塑造内容、二维图像、虚拟漫游、三维模型、研究论著等数字资料进行整合，使其能够在基于互联网的使用平台上达到共享，同时追求各方位的水陆庵泥塑资料不受时间和空间限制服务于大众，从而可对文物的管理、研究、保护、交流、教育等产生积极的推进作用。

Ⅴ. Wed-based Data Integration and Sharing

　　At present, the Internet has become the main channel for global information sharing. Because of the unique characteristics of cultural objects, their "digitization" inevitably generates enormous quantities of information. The bottleneck in the use and transmission of information from cultural objects lies in the problem of how to allow users to conveniently access various types of information online. In this project, the tremendous volume of information generated about the Shuilu'an Temple--the historical background of the building and sculptures, the contents of the sculptures, 2D images, VR's, 3D models and research articles--had to be integrated and organized so that they could be shared across an Internet-based platform. Another goal was to allow users to access the Shuilu'an materials at any time and from any location, so as to facilitate their use for management, research, conservation, exchanges and education in the field of cultural relics.

118   水陆庵项目网页：三维导航页
Shuilu'an project Web site：3D navigation page

119   水陆庵项目网页：高清晰二维图像浏览页
Shuilu'an project Web site：browser page for high-resolution 2D images

120 水陆庵项目网页：单墙面元数据页
Shuilu'an project Web site：metadata page for single wall

121 水陆庵项目网页：高清晰二维图像浏览页内容注解功能
Shuilu'an project Web site：content annotation function within browser page for high-resolution 2D images

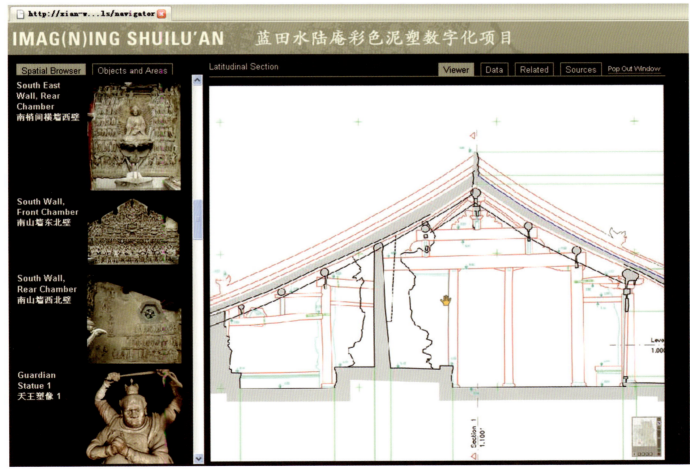

122　水陆庵项目网页：高清晰二维图像浏览页局部缩放功能

Shuilu'an project Web site：zooming function within browser page for high-resolution 2D images

123　水陆庵项目网页：三维测量剖面页

Shuilu'an project Web site：sectional drawing page from 3D measurements

124　水陆庵项目网页：虚拟漫游展播页
　　　　Shuilu'an project Web site：VR display page

125　水陆庵项目网页：三维模型展播页
　　　　Shuilu'an project Web site：3D model display page

[附 录]

一　项目大事记

2003 年 9 月 2 日	中国陕西省文物局局长张廷皓、局外事处处长李斌，西安文物保护修复中心副主任王道武研究员与美国西北大学学术技术部先进媒体制作室主任哈伦·瓦拉克（万里）先生和美国梅隆基金会代表梅缵月女士，考察了"蓝田水陆庵彩色泥塑"、"陕西省考古研究所安伽墓文物"、"陕西历史博物馆唐墓壁画"，就《文物的高清晰度数字化图像》合作项目进行调查选项。之后，美方代表向梅隆基金会项目主管华特斯先生提交有关合作选项的报告。
2003 年 9 月 4 日	西安文物保护修复中心向陕西省文物局和美国梅隆基金会申请开展《三维扫描及数字化图像制作技术在蓝田水陆庵的应用研究》项目。
2003 年 10 月 13 日	美国梅隆基金会项目主管官员华特斯先生现场考察蓝田水陆庵彩色泥塑以后，与陕西省文物局局长张廷皓，省文物局外事处处长李斌、文物处处长周魁英和西安文物保护修复中心领导侯卫东、王道武、齐扬座谈，确定推行水陆庵数字图像合作项目的可行性。
2004 年 3 月 27 日	美国西北大学向梅隆基金会申请用于探讨大型数字化项目可行性的机动拨款，申请书题为《为高清晰摄影技术的支持、培训和传播，以及为对甘肃、山西两省塑像进行三维采集的研究》。本次申请的目的是继续与上述技术有关的培训合作，以及为进一步探讨高清晰彩色泥塑图像采集与三维结构图像采集之间的关系提供初步的支持。
2004 年 5 月 28 日	美国梅隆基金会正式同意资助《三维扫描及数字化图像制作技术在蓝田水陆庵的应用研究》项目。
2004 年 6 月 3 日	经报国家文物局同意后，西安文物保护修复中心王道武、阎敏赴山西省文物局，调用美国梅隆基金会援助、美国西北大学支持的早期数字化摄影项目所使用过的台架及部分器材，双方进行了移交。调用的器材移交西安文物

保护修复中心并制作了专用箱保管。

2004 年 6 月 10 日　　中美双方通过邮件确认了前期技术培训和现场试拍摄的
　　　　　　　　　　设备器材情况，对缺少的进行了补充。

2004 年 6 月 21 日　　西安文物保护修复中心王道武、王展赴甘肃敦煌调研，
　　　　　　　　　　学习敦煌研究院与美国梅隆基金会合作的高清晰度数字
　　　　　　　　　　化图像合作项目。

2004 年 6 月 28 日　　西安文物保护修复中心研究决定，成立了中美合作数
　　　　　　　　　　字化图像项目组，并报省文物局。组长王道武，成员王
　　　　　　　　　　展、杨宝贵、甄刚、李博。

2004 年 7 月 6 日　　美国哈伦·瓦拉克（万里）等专家在西安对中方技术
　　　　　　　　　　人员进行两天的前期技术培训。

2004 年 7 月 8 日　　美国万里等专家和中方技术人员在蓝田水陆庵现场进
　　　　　　　　　　行了两天试验拍摄。

2004 年 8～10 月　　对蓝田水陆庵水陆殿内的北山墙壁塑试拍摄的图像进
　　　　　　　　　　行后期处理制作。

2004 年 11 月 15 日　美国万里等专家来陕两天，对试验拍摄工作进行了小
　　　　　　　　　　结，对进一步的开展合作进行了计划，双方开始起草合
　　　　　　　　　　作协议文本。

2005 年 1～9 月　　正式向中国国家文物局、陕西省文物局、西安市文物
　　　　　　　　　　局上报合作项目申请文件和合作协议文本。

2005 年 3 月 25 日　　美国西北大学向梅隆基金会提交有关机动拨款工作成
　　　　　　　　　　功完成的最后报告。

2005 年 6 月 30 日　　美国西北大学万里向梅隆基金会提交题为《想"像"水
　　　　　　　　　　陆庵》即《三维扫描及数字化图像制作技术在蓝田水陆
　　　　　　　　　　庵的应用研究》的申请书，要求基金会支持美国西北大
　　　　　　　　　　学和中国西安文物保护修复中心的合作图像制作项目。
　　　　　　　　　　本项目提出要对蓝田水陆庵殿内的全部彩色泥塑进行高
　　　　　　　　　　清晰图像拍摄和制作，与此同时对水陆庵的局部进行试

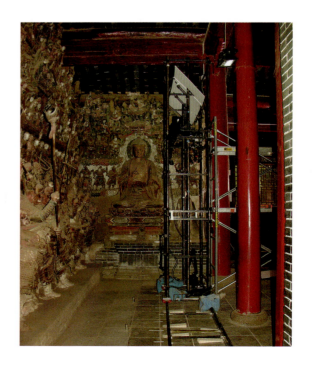

验性的三维数据采集和制作。此外，工作计划也包括相关的软件开发。

2005 年 9 月 2 日	中国国家文物局批复（文物保函[2005]1008 号）同意此合作项目的开展。
2005 年 9 月 8 日	美国梅隆基金会法定代表人威廉·保文和西安文物保护修复中心法定代表人侯卫东主任签署正式合作协议。
2005 年 9 月 19 日	陕西省文物局、西安市文物局批复同意此合作项目的开始实施。
2005 年 9 月 19 日	美国梅隆基金会同意拨款支持美国西北大学《想"像"水陆庵》即《三维扫描及数字化图像制作技术在蓝田水陆庵的应用研究》的申请。
2005 年 9 月	陕西省文物局拨付部分配套经费。
2005 年 9 月 25 日	西安文物保护修复中心、西安市文物局、蓝田县文物旅游局、水陆庵文物管理所的领导和中方项目组召开协调会议，研究落实项目的实施方案，会议由侯卫东主持。
2005 年 10～12 月	完成蓝田水陆庵数字化正式拍摄的各项准备工作，美国专家携带大量的数字化先进器材到西安。
2005 年 10 月 14 日	中美项目组赴蓝田水陆庵，全面开始了二维高清晰数字摄影、虚拟漫游、三维测量测绘、三维扫描工作。先后有中外专家三十余人次，历时三个月，在现场开展工作。双方专家克服困难、齐心协力、精益求精地完成了前期的现场拍摄任务。 工作期间，得到蓝田县文物旅游局、水陆庵文物管理所的大力配合支持。陕西省文物局、西安文物保护修复中心和敦煌研究院的领导到现场检查指导工作。敦煌研究院数字化中心主任刘刚、摄影师孙洪才受邀协助工作。
2006 年 1～12 月	进行二维高清晰数字摄影、虚拟漫游、三维测量测绘、三维扫描后期制作处理、元数据收集整理及数据库建设。

2006 年 5 月 12 日	后期处理及数据库建设。中美项目组召开第一次业务电话会议，统一思想，统一技术路线。
2006 年 6 月 16 日	后期处理及数据库建设。中美项目组召开第二次业务电话会议，研究解决技术问题。
2006 年 7 月 19 日	美国万里等专家来陕四天。中美项目组对前一阶段的合作进行了小结，讨论数据库建设和元数据输入等问题。西安文物保护修复中心领导侯卫东、齐扬参加会议，研究和解决问题。
2006 年 8 月	中方项目组王道武、王展开始调查、收集、整理和输入元数据。蓝田县周启民、樊维岳、张卫军等给予支持和帮助。
2006 年 9 月	中方项目组向陕西省文物局局长赵荣等领导专题汇报了《蓝田水陆庵数字化图像制作技术的应用研究》项目的初步成果，局长赵荣等领导作了重要指示。
2006 年 10 月	中方项目组分别向中国国家文物局数字化信息委员会会议、陕西省文物局直属文博单位文物数字化工作会议汇报《蓝田水陆庵数字化图像制作技术的应用研究》项目的初步成果，受到领导和专家的好评。
2006 年 11 月 28 日	美国万里、奥地利林星格等专家来陕五天。中美双方对前一阶段的工作进行了总结汇报，陕西省文物局副局长刘云辉、文物处处长周魁英、文物专家孔昱及西安文物保护修复中心的领导侯卫东、齐扬、马涛等听取了汇报，肯定了合作取得的成绩，并对今后开展新的合作提出了指导性意见。 同时，美国和奥地利专家就水陆庵合作项目中采用的各项数字化技术，对中方人员进行了全面的技术辅导。
2006 年 11 月 29 日	双方讨论了此次合作成果的技术推广和应用（出版本次合作成果和考察新的合作项目）达成初步意见，并对项

目总结汇报及评审会的有关事项进行了研究和安排。

2006 年 12 月 21 日 陕西省文物局局长赵荣在发表的《增强科学意识，运用科学技术，积极促进和提升文化遗产保护科技水平》文章中指出：中美合作"运用二维高清晰度拍摄与拼接技术和高分辨率三维数字化建模技术，对水陆庵泥塑进行全息信息采集，最高分辨 0.1 毫米，在国内处于领先地位"。

2007 年 5 月 21~23 日 项目总结和评审会议在西安召开，中美合作项目的中方项目组组长王道武研究员，美方项目负责人哈伦·瓦拉克媒体技术设计师先后对项目的概况、应用技术及成果等进行了汇报、展示和答疑。

参加会议的中美专家组成专家评审委员会，对项目成果进行了评审。

中国国家文物局、陕西省文物局和美国西北大学的领导参加了会议，并作了重要讲话。

2007 年 5 月 23 日 举行了合作项目成果的移交仪式。西安文物保护修复中心主任侯卫东和美方代表西北大学马丁·缪勒教授分别代表合作双方签字。专家评审委员会主任张廷皓研究员宣读了专家评审结论，陕西省文物局刘云辉副局长、美国西北大学马丁·缪勒教授分别发表了热情洋溢的讲话，对会议的成功表示祝贺，并期望今后继续开展合作。

2007 年 5 月 24 日 中美专家考察了乾陵、茂陵和公输堂。

[Appendices]

I . Project Chronology

September 2, 2003	Zhang Tinghao, Director of the Shaanxi Provincial Bureau of Cultural Relics, Li Bin, head of the Bureau's Department of External Affairs, and Wang Daowu, deputy director and a research fellow of the Xi'an Center for the Conservation and Restoration of Cultural Relics, meet with Harlan Wallach, Director of NUAMPS, department of Academic Technologies, Northwestern University, and June Mei, representing the Andrew W. Mellon Foundation of the U.S.A. They examined the clay sculptures of the Shuilu'an, the relics of the tomb of Anjia in the Shaanxi Institute of Archaeology, and the Tang dynasty tomb murals in the Shaanxi Provincial Historical Museum, to explore possibilities for a cooperative project on the high-resolution digitization of cultural relics. A report on the possible options for a cooperative effort was then submitted by the Americans to Don Waters, program officer of the Andrew W. Mellon Foundation of the U.S.A.
September 4, 2003	The Xi'an Center for the Conservation and Restoration of Cultural Relics makes a request to the Shaanxi Provincial Bureau of Cultural Relics and to the Andrew W. Mellon Foundation to initiate a project on the "Applications of 3D scanning and digital image production technology at the Shuilu'an Temple in Lantian".
October 13, 2003	After a site visit to see the clay sculptures in the Shuilu'an, Mr. Don Waters, Program Officer of the Andrew W. Mellon Foundation, meets with Zhang Tinghao, Director of the Shaanxi Provincial Bureau of Cultural Relics, representatives of the relevant offices of the Bureau, and with leaders of the Xi'an Center for the Conservation and Restoration of Cultural Relics to confirm the possibilities of moving forward with a project.
March 27, 2004	An officers grant application to explore feasibility of a larger digitization and implementation grant is submitted to the the Andrew W. Mellon Foundation by Northwestern University. The application is titled "Support, training and dispersal of high-resolution photographic techniques, and research towards initiating three-dimensional capture of sculptural objects in Gansu and Shaanxi Province, China." The goal of this grant application was to continue the educational collaboration associated with development of these techniques and provide initial support for further exploration of the relationship between the acquisition of high-resolution surface textures and three-dimensional structures of the painted clay sculptures.
May 28, 2004	The Andrew W. Mellon Foundation formally agrees to support the project on "Applications of 3D scanning and digital image production technology at the Shuilu'an Temple in Lantian."
June 3, 2004	With approval from the National Administration of Cultural heritage, Wang Daowu and Yan Min of the Xi'an Center for the Conservation and Restoration of Cultural Relics go to Shanxi Province to transport the rig and some of the equipment used in an earlier project on digital photography which

	was supported by Northwestern University in a project funded by the Andrew W. Mellon foundation.
June 10, 2004	Through an exchange of e-mails, the Chinese and American sides confirm the equipment list required for preliminary technical training and for on-site photography, and add components to make up for some shortages.
June 21, 2004	Wang Daowu and Wang Zhan of the Xi'an Center for the Conservation and Restoration of Cultural Relics go to Dunhuang to learn about the cooperative project on high-resolution digitization there between the Andrew W. Mellon Foundation and the Dunhuang Research Academy.
June 28, 2004	The Xi'an Center for the Conservation and Restoration of Cultural Relics establishes its project team for the Sino-American joint project on digital imaging.Team leader: Wang Daowu.Team members: Wang Zhan, Yang Guibao, Zhen Gang and Li Bo. This is reported to the provincial Bureau of Cultural Relics.
July 6, 2004	Harlan Wallach of Northwestern University and other specialists conduct two days of preliminary training in Xi'an for the Chinese technical staff.
July 8, 2004	Harlan Wallach of Northwestern University and other specialists and the Chinese technical staff conduct two days of on-site experimental photography at the Shuilu'an in Lantian.
August to October, 2004	Processing of part of the images from the experimental photography of the interior north wall of the Shuilu Pavilion.
November 15, 2004	Harlan Wallach and other specialists spend four days in Shaanxi to sum up the results of the experimental photography, and to further lay out plans for the collaboration. Both sides begin to draft the text of an agreement.
January to September, 2005	Application documents and the text of the agreement on collaboration are formally submitted to the State　Administration of Cultural Heritage, the Shaanxi Provincial Bureau of Cultural Relics and the Xi'an Municipal Bureau of Cultural Relics.
March 25, 2005	A final report on the successful result of the Officers Grant is submitted to the Andrew W. Mellon Foundation by Northwestern University.
June 30, 2005	An imaging and digitization grant proposal titled "Imag(n)ing Shuilu'an: Applications of 3D scanning and digital image production technology at the Shuilu'an Temple in Lantian" is submitted to the Andrew W. Mellon foundation by Harlan Wallach of Northwestern University to provide support for a collaborative imaging project between Northwestern University and the Xi'an Center for the Conservation and Restoration of Cultural Relics. This imaging project proposed to completely document in high-resolution digital imagery the interior of the Shuilu'an Temple, Lantian, Xi'an, China. A parallel effort to the imaging of the temple is an experimental acquisition of a partial 3D

dataset. The work plan also includes development of related software.

September 2, 2005　　The State Administration of Cultural Heritage gives approval for the commencement of this collaborative project.

September 8, 2005　　William G. Bowen, legal representative of the Andrew W. Mellon Foundation, and Hou Weidong, legal representative of the Xi'an Center for the Conservation and Restoration of Cultural Relics, execute the official agreement.

September 19, 2005　　The Shaanxi Provincial Bureau of Cultural Relics and the Xi'an Municipal Bureau of Cultural Relics give approvals for the commencement and implementation of this collaborative project.

September 19, 2005　　The Andrew W. Mellon Foundation approves the grant request from Northwestern University for "Imag(n)ing Shuiluan: Applications of 3D scanning and digital image production technology at the Shuilu'an Temple in Lantian".

September, 2005　　The Shaanxi Provincial Bureau of Cultural Relics approves a grant for project expenses.

September 25, 2005　　Leaders of the Xi'an Center for the Conservation and Restoration of Cultural Relics, the Xi'an Municipal Bureau of Cultural Relics, the Lantian County Office of Cultural Relics and Tourism, the Shuilu'an Office of Cultural Relics Management, and the Chinese project team convene a coordination meeting to study project implementation and execution plans.

October to December, 2005　　After completion of all preparatory work for the digital photography at Shuilu'an, the American specialists bring a large quantity of advanced equipment.

October 14, 2005　　The Chinese and American project teams go to Shuilu'an and commence work on 2D high-resolution digital photography, VR's, 3D surveying and measuring, and 3D scanning. This requires some 30+ person-trips for on-site work by Chinese and foreign experts.

With the strong support of the Lantian County Office of Cultural Relics and Tourism and the Shuilu'an Office of Cultural Relics Management, on site work continues for three months. During this time, leaders from the Shaanxi Provincial Bureau of Cultural Relics and the Xi'an Center for the Conservation and Restoration of Cultural Relics, as well as leaders from the Dunhuang Research Academy, visit the site to inspect and to offer guidance for the ongoing work. Liu Gang, director of the Digitization Center of the Dunhuang Research Academy, and photographer Sun Hongcai assist in the work.

January to December, 2006　　Postproduction work on 2D high-resolution photography, VR's, 3D surveys and measurements, and 3D scanning; collection of metadata; establishment of database.

May 12, 2006　　First working conference call between the Chinese and American project teams regarding postproduction and database development, to ensure coordination of concepts and technical paths. The image annotator developed by Northwestern University is presented.

June 13, 2006
Second working conference call between the Chinese and American project teams regarding postproduction and database development, to explore solutions to technical problems.

July 19, 2006
Harlan Wallach and other specialists come to Shaanxi for four days. The Chinese and American project teams summarize the work done in the previous phase, and discuss the development of the database and metadata input. Hou Weidong and Qi Yang, leaders of the Xi'an Center for the Conservation and Restoration of Cultural Relics, participate in the discussions and resolution of problems.

August 2006
Wang Daowu and Wang Zhan of the Chinese project team begin to research, collect, organize and input metadata. Zhou Qimin, Fan Weiyue and Zhang Weijun of Lantian County provide support and assistance.

September 2006
The Chinese project team reports to Director Zhao Rong and other leaders of the Shaanxi Provincial Bureau of Relics on the preliminary results of the project "Applications of 3D scanning and digital image production technology at the Shuilu'an Temple in Lantian." Director Zhao and others give important instructions.

October 2006
The Chinese project team makes reports on the preliminary results of the project at a conference of the digital information committee of the State Administration of Cultural Heritage, and at a working conference on cultural relics digitization work of relics institutions and museums under the direct jurisdiction of the Shaanxi provincial Bureau of Relics. The reports are very favorably received by leaders and experts.

November 28, 2006
Harlan Wallach of Northwestern University, U.S.A, Stefan Linsinger of Austria, and other experts come to Shaanxi for five days. The Chinese and American sides sum up the previous stage of work, and give a comprehensive technical report on the various digitization techniques used at Shuilu'an for the Chinese side. Liu Yunhui, Vice director of the provincial Bureau of Relics, Zhou Kuiying, head of the Relics Department of the Bureau, relics specialist Kong Yu, and Hou Weidong, Qi Yang and Ma Tao, leaders the Xi'an Center for the Conservation and Restoration of Cultural Relics hear the reports, affirm the results of this collaboration, and offer guidance on initiating new collaboration in the future.

November 29, 2006
Both sides come to some preliminary conclusions on the dissemination and application of the results achieved through this collaboration, on the publication of the project's results, and on exploring a new joint project. They also discuss organizing a conference to report on the project results, as well as an evaluation session.

December 21, 2006
Zhao Rong, Director of the Shaanxi Provincial Bureau of Cultural Relics, publishes an article

entitled "Heighten scientific awareness, utilize science and technology, promote and elevate the scientific and technological level of heritage conservation." In it, he points out that the Sino-American collaboration "utilized 2D high resolution photography and stitching and high resolution 3D digital modeling to capture comprehensive information from the Shuilu'an sculptures. The highest resolution achieved was 0.1 mm, which is pacesetting within China."

May 21～23, 2007   A project summation and evaluation conference was convened in Xi'an. Chinese team leader Prof. Wang Daowu and American team leader Media Architect Harlan Wallach reported on the project, the technologies applied and its results, gave demonstrations and answered questions. An evaluation committee composed of Chinese and American specialists attended the conference and assessed the results of the project.

Important remarks were made by leading representatives of the State Administration of Cultural Heritage, the Shaanxi Provincial Bureau of Cultural Relics and Northwestern University.

May 23,2007   The project results were handed over in a transfer ceremony. Hou Weidong, director of the Xi'an Center for the Conservation and Restoration of Cultural Relics, and Prof. Martin Mueller of Northwestern University signed the papers on behalf of the collaborating partners. Co-chairman Prof. Zhang Tinghao of the evaluation committee read a summary of the committee's assessment. Warm remarks were given by Liu Yunhui, Deputy Director of the Shaanxi Provincial Bureau of Cultural Relics and Prof. Martin Mueller of Northwestern University, congratulating the conference on its success and expressing wishes for continuing cooperation.

May 24, 2007   Chinese and American experts made a working visit to Qianling, Maoling and Gongshutang.

二　项目评审简报

2007年5月21～23日，中国陕西省文物局在西安主持召开了中美合作《三维扫描及数字化图像制作技术在蓝田水陆庵的应用研究》项目总结、评审会议。

会议由陕西省文物局文物处处长周魁英主持。西安文物保护修复中心侯卫东主任致欢迎词，刘云辉副局长、宋新潮司长分别代表陕西省文物局和中国国家文物局做了重要讲话。梅缵月和马丁·缪勒分别宣读了美国梅隆基金会前会长、ARTstor主席威廉·保文和梅隆基金会项目主管唐·沃特斯及美国西北大学校长亨利·彼能对合作项目获得成功的祝贺词。

会议推选中国文物研究所所长（现中国文化遗产研究院院长）张廷皓和美国西北大学技术部主任罗伯特·泰勒为评审专家委员会主任，美国西北大学温伯格文理学院教授马丁·缪勒为评审专家委员会协调员。评审会议由张廷皓先生和罗伯特·泰勒先生共同主持。

中美合作项目的中方项目组组长王道武研究员，美方项目负责人哈伦·瓦拉克媒体技术设计师先后对项目的概况、应用技术及成果等进行了汇报、展示和答疑。

与会的领导和专家对项目取得的成果，先进的文物数字化技术的开发和应用进行了充分的肯定和较高的评价。专家委员会经过充分讨论、认真评议，一致认为：

1．中美合作项目选择的应用对象具有针对性，对此类文物进行高清晰图像的采集、制作和存储具有一定的指导意义。通过成功高效的组织、友好的合作、精心的工作，全面完成了合作协议的目标和任务。

2．中美合作项目对多层空间、细节丰富、结构和布局复杂、面积巨大的彩色泥质雕塑、壁塑、悬塑群，进行二维高清晰图像的采集、制作和存储，解决了拍摄和后期处理的许多难点，文物图像的清晰度和分辨率之高在国内外当属首次。多种技术的综合应用，尤其是在三维扫描、三维测量测绘建模技术的基础上，综合使用了多种数据、不同种类、海量文物信息数据的存储和有效的使用。创新开发的新的浏览及注释工具，实现了跨国界、多地域、多用户对项目产生的各种成果在不同领域、不同层次的充分应用。这是数字技术在文物研究应用上的突破。

3．中美合作项目建立的基于Internet的文字、2D图像、3D模型等数据信息的综合信息平台，可全面地使用多种资料对文物进行研究、保护、交流、宣传等。

4．中美合作项目使用的三维扫描技术选择在水陆庵泥塑的应用尝试，对该项技术在文物领域的应用具有深远的意义，项目中使用的各种技术在文化遗产应用中有很好的示范性。

中美专家对项目产生的各种图像及数据，在宣传、教育、考古、古建、美术及文物研究和保护等方面的应用和推广，提出以下建议：

1．西安文物保护修复中心、敦煌研究院和美国西北大学应共同对《二维高清晰图像的拍摄和制作技术的应用》申报科技进步奖，以便更好的推广该项目的成果。

2．充分利用该项目的成果，加强与保护修复技术、考古技术等的切入和关联，提高文物的保护和考古研究的数字化水平。特别是水陆庵彩色泥塑群完整的二维高清晰图像，开展水陆庵泥塑的历史、宗教及工艺美术史、绘画艺术、雕塑技术等多方面的研究，可就相关的数字化研究项目向国家、省市有关部门申请立项支持和经费保障。

3．进一步完善已有软件和设备器材，提高人机互动性和使用便捷性，为该项目成果更为广泛推广和应用提供良好的条件。

评议专家组一致认为本项目达到了预期目标，同意通过评审，提交验收。

参加评议会议的专家有中国文物研究所所长（现中国文化遗产研究院院长）张廷皓，美国西北大学学术技术部主任罗伯特·泰勒、美国西北大学教授马丁·缪勒，东南大学副教授胡明星，国家文物局文物鉴定陕西分站站长呼林贵，陕西省考古研究所副所长张建林，西安美术学院教授王宁宇，中国文物信息咨询中心信息部主任陈刚。

特邀专家西安市文物局副局长向德，敦煌研究院文物信息中心主任刘刚，西安文物保护修复中心总工程师马涛、秦建明，安德鲁·W·梅隆基金会顾问兼项目协调人梅缵月，美国西北大学三维模型专家兼制作助理罗兰·霍丽戴，陕西省文物局文物处副处长孔昱，蓝田文物旅游局文物科长杨有勤，蓝田水陆庵文管所所长张卫军、副所长赵亮参加了会议。中美双方的项目组成员同时与会。

专家评审会议后，5月23日下午，举行了项目成果的移交仪式。仪式由陕西省文物局文物处副处长孔昱主持，西安文物保护修复中心主任侯卫东和美方代表马丁·缪勒教授分别代表合作双方签字。评审专家委员会主任张廷皓研究员宣读了专家评审结果，陕西省文物局刘云辉副局长、美国西北大学马丁·缪勒教授分别发表了热情洋溢的讲话，对会议的成功表示祝贺，并期望今后继续开展合作。

II. Project Evaluation Report

On May 21 ~ 23, 2007, the Shaanxi Provincial Bureau of Cultural Relics convened a conference to summarize and evaluate the project "Applications of 3D scanning and digital image production technology at the Shuilu'an Temple in Lantian."

The meeting was chaired by Zhou Kuiying, Director of the Division of Cultural Relics of the Shaanxi Provincial Bureau of Cultural Relics. A welcoming speech was made by Hou Weidong, director of the Xi'an Center for the Conservation and Restoration of Cultural Relics, and important remarks were delivered by Deputy Bureau Director Liu Yunhui and Department Director Song Xinchao on behalf of the Shaanxi Provincial Bureau of Cultural Relics and the State Administration of Cultural Heritage respectively. Congratulatory messages from William Bowen, former President of the Andrew W. Mellon Foundation and Chairman of ARTstor, Donald J. Waters, Program Officer of the Andrew W. Mellon Foundation, and President Henry Bienen of Northwestern University were read on their behalf by Ms. June Mei and Prof. Martin Mueller.

Zhang Tinghao, Director of the China Cultural Relics Research Institute (now the China Academy for Cultural Heritage Studies), and Prof. Martin Mueller of the Weinberg College of Arts and Sciences of Northwestern University were elected by the attendees to be co-coordinators of the evaluation committee. The evaluation meeting was co-chaired by Zhang Tinghao and Robert Taylor.

Chinese team leader Prof. Wang Daowu and American team leader Media Architect Harlan Wallach reported on the project, the technologies applied and its results, gave demonstrations and answered questions.

The attending leaders and experts gave a favorable opinion and high assessment of the project's outcomes, of the advanced heritage digitization technologies developed and of their application. After thorough discussion and careful evaluation, it was unanimously agreed that:

1. The site of the project was well selected, and there is ground-breaking significance in capturing, producing and storing high resolution images of such cultural relics. Through successful and efficient organization, friendly cooperation and meticulous work, all the goals laid out in the agreement of collaboration were achieved.

2. This Sino-American collaborative project captured, produced and stored 2D high resolution images of clay sculptures in the round, wall sculptures and hanging sculptures. These occupied many spatial layers, were highly detailed, complex in composition and layout, and covered a large area. In the course of this work, many difficulties in photography and postproduction were resolved. The definition and resolution of the images are cutting-edge both inside and outside China. There was an integrated use of many kinds of technologies, particularly in the integrated storage and use of many types and huge quantities of different types of data and information which were based on models derived from 3D scanning and surveying. New browsing and notation tools were developed which can be by accessed by multiple users across national borders and regions to fully utilize the many types of project outcomes at many levels and for different purposes. This is a breakthrough in the application of digital technologies to the study of cultural relics.

3. This Sino-American collaborative project has created an integrated Internet-based information platform which

brings together text, 2D images and 3D models. This allows the full use of many types of materials for research, conservation, exchanges and dissemination in cultural heritage work.

4. The choice of 3D scanning technologies chosen by this Sino-American collaborative project for experimental use on the Shuilu'an clay sculptures has great significance for the application of such technologies on cultural relics, and the various technologies employed in the project set an excellent example for applications to cultural heritage work.

Regarding the uses and promotion of the images and data generated by the project for dissemination, education, archeology, ancient architecture, art, heritage studies and conservation, the Chinese and American experts made the following recommendations:

1. The Xi'an Center for the Conservation and Restoration of Cultural Relics, Dunhuang Academy and Northwestern University Department of Academic Technologies (NUAMPS) should jointly submit the project "Applications of 3D scanning and digital image production technology at the Shuilu'an Temple in Lantian" for consideration for a science and technology prize, so that the project results can become better known.

2. The project results should be more fully utilized by employing them in conservation and repair efforts and archeological techniques, and using them to raise digitization standards in conservation and archeological research. In particular, the complete set of 2D high resolution images of the Shuilu'an clay sculptures should be used to initiate studies on the history of the sculptures, as well as research in other areas including history of religion, history of arts and crafts, history of painting and sculpting, etc. Applications should be submitted to the appropriate agencies of the national and local governments for funding for digitization research.

3. The existing software and hardware should be improved in order to further enhance interactivity and ease of use, so that project results can be more widely disseminated and utilized.

The members of the evaluation committee unanimously agreed that the project achieved its goals. The evaluation report was passed and submitted for acceptance.

The experts sitting on the evaluation committee were: Zhang Tinghao, Director of the China Cultural Relics Research Institute (now the China Academy for Cultural Heritage Studies); Prof. Robert Taylor, Director of the Northwestern University Department of Academic Technologies; Prof. Martin Mueller of Northwestern University; Associate Prof. Hu Mingxing of Southeastern University; Research Prof. Hu Lingui, Director of the Shaanxi office of the State Administration of Cultural Heritage's Cultural Relics Authentication Division; Prof. Wang Ningyu of the Xi'an Art Academy; and Research Prof. Chen Gang, Director of the Information Division of the China Center for Cultural Relics Information and Consultation.

Specially invited attendees were: Research Prof. Xiang De, Deputy Director of the Xi'an Municipal Department of Cultural Relics; Prof. Liu Gang, Director of the Information Center of the Dunhuang Academy; Research Prof. Ma Tao, Chief Engineer of The Xi'an Center for the Conservation and Restoration of Cultural Relics; Research Prof. Qin Jianming of The Xi'an Center for the Conservation and Restoration of Cultural Relics; June Y. Mei, Consultant and Project Facilitator of the Andrew W. Mellon Foundation; Lauren Holliday, 3D modeling specialist and production assistant, Northwestern University; Kong Yu, Deputy Chief of the Cultural Relics Section, Shaanxi Provincial Bureau of Cultural Relics; Yang Youqin, Director of the Cultural Relics Division, Lantian County Department of Cultural Relics and Tourism; Zhang Weijun, Director, and Zhao Liang, Deputy Director, of the Shuilu'an Office of Cultural Relics Management.

The members of the Chinese and American project teams also attended the meetings.

On the afternoon of May 23, after the conclusion of the evaluation meeting, a ceremony for the transfer of project outcomes was held. It was presided over by Kong Yu, Deputy Chief of the Cultural Relics Section, Shaanxi Provincial Bureau of Cultural Relics, and the documents were signed by Hou Weidong, Director of the Xi'an Center for the Conservation and Restoration of Cultural Relics, and Prof. Martin Mueller of Northwestern University on behalf of the two collaborating parties. Zhang Tinghao, Co-Chairman of the Evaluation Committee, read the results of the assessment. Warm remarks congratulating the conference on its success and wishing for continuing collaboration were offered by Liu Yunhui, Deputy Director of the Shaanxi Provincial Bureau of Cultural Relics and by Prof. Martin Mueller.

后　记

　　水陆庵彩绘泥塑数字化合作项目历经几年努力，于2007年圆满完成。在得到了上级及各方专家的好评的同时，我们担忧项目使用的技术和高质量的影像被置之高阁，特别期望将其以更直观的图书形式展现出来，广泛服务于文博事业。可喜的是，在基金会和上级主管部门的支持下，可以将之呈现于世。自2007年以来，经中国西安文物保护修复中心、美国西北大学学术技术部和文物出版社积极配合，终将利用计算机展示的数字技术及影像汇集成册。现本书即将付梓出版，但愿以此促进文化遗产保护数字化技术应用及水陆庵泥塑的研究、保护、交流和宣传。

　　如大事记载述，合作的成功有赖于国家文物局、陕西省文物局的组织和领导，西安市文物局、蓝田县文物旅游局、水陆庵文物管理所、敦煌研究院、美国梅隆基金会、美国西北大学及美国西北大学学术技术部的大力配合和支持。在项目实施中，蓝田县文物旅游局副局长周启民，蓝田水陆庵文物管理所所长张卫军、副所长赵亮、原所长樊维岳，敦煌研究院文物信息中心主任刘刚、摄影师孙洪才等在设备提供和资料整理等方面给予很大的协助。中国西安文物保护修复中心陈军、冯俊忠、王建龙等同仁在后勤服务、财务管理给予帮助，在此一并致谢。

　　另外，本书的编排得到了文物出版社总编辑葛承雍的大力协助，在此诚擎致谢。

　　本书的内容旨在重点展示水陆庵项目使用技术及影像成果，仅就水陆庵泥塑的其他方面只是简单注释，以作抛砖之引玉，期盼利用此次合作成果为水陆庵彩绘泥塑研究的相关论著锦上添花。

编　者

2009 年 6 月 11 日

Editor's Postscript

After several years of work, the collaborative project to create digital images of the painted clay sculptures at the Shuilu'an Temple was successfully concluded in 2007. It was favorably reviewed by overseeing agencies and by experts in the field; at the same time, we particularly hoped to present the technologies used and the high-quality images created in the more palpable form of a book, so that they could be more broadly available for cultural and conservation projects. Our concern was that these technologies and images would simply gather dust. Fortunately, with the support of the Mellon Foundation and our supervisory agencies, we have been able to compile and publish such a book. Since 2007, the Xi'an Center for the Conservation and Restoration of Cultural Relics, the Northwestern University Department of Academic & Research Technologies and the Cultural Relics Press have worked together closely and are now finally able to publish some of the computer-processed digital data and images. As this work goes to press, we express here our hope that it will further promote the application of digital technologies to cultural conservation work, and that it will facilitate research, conservation, exchanges and publicizing of the clay sculptures at Shuilu'an.

As described in the chronology, the success of our collaboration was made possible by the organization and leadership of the State Administration of Cultural Heritage and the Shaanxi Provincial Bureau of Cultural Relics, and by the close coordination and support of the Xi'an Municipal Bureau of Cultural Relics, the Lantian County Office of Cultural Relics and Tourism, the Shuilu'an Office of Cultural Relics Management, the Dunhuang Academy, the Andrew W. Mellon Foundation, Northwestern University and the Northwestern University Department of Academic & Research Technologies. During the course of the project's implementation, we received a tremendous amount of assistance with equipment and research materials from Zhou Qimin, Deputy Director of the Lantian County Office of Cultural Relics and Tourism, Zhang Weijun, Director, Zhao Liang, Deputy Director, and former Director Fan Weiyue of the Shuilu'an Office of Cultural Relics Management, Liu Gang, Director of the Dunhuang Academy's Digitization Center and Sun Hongcai, Dunhuang Academy photographer. Our colleagues Chen Jun, Feng Junzhong and Wang Jianlong of the Xi'an Center for the Conservation and Restoration of Cultural Relics assisted us in logistics and bookkeeping. To all of them we express our heartfelt thanks.

We are also most grateful to Ge Chengyong, Editor-in-Chief of the Cultural Relics Press, who helped greatly with the book's layout.

The book's focus is on the technologies used in the Shuilu'an project and the images thus created, hence other aspects of the Shuilu'an clay sculptures are only simply annotated. Our hope is that this humble beginning can lead to greater results, and that the fruits of this collaboration will augment future research on the sculptures.

June 11, 2009